CHARACTER-BUILDING STUFF

DECLAN SHORTHALL

authorHOUSE®

AuthorHouse™
1663 Liberty Drive
Bloomington, IN 47403
www.authorhouse.com
Phone: 1-800-839-8640

Published by AuthorHouse   06/26/2012

ISBN: 978-1-4772-1433-6 (sc)
ISBN: 978-1-4772-1434-3 (hc)
ISBN: 978-1-4772-1435-0 (e)

INTRODUCTION

PEOPLE HAVE BEEN suggesting that I write a book about my life for several years now. However, I have never really known where to start. But so much has happened over the past four or five years that I now feel compelled to write something. So I shall begin by giving you a little information about myself.

I am currently thirty-seven years old. I have been married to my wife Lisa for fifteen years, and we have three wonderful children. We live in a council house in a lovely picturesque village in Somerset, England. I will not mention what stage of my life I am in at the moment, as I feel it may not be the right time.

One of the main reasons I am writing this book is to try and counter the popular view of young people as being unsalable or irredeemable. It is a fact that many young people who become involved in antisocial or criminal behavior do tend to continue this behavior into their adult lives, but life, as we all know, is constantly changing and never predictable. Even the most secure employment is at risk during a recession, and marriages are forever falling apart with at least one person involved oblivious to the fact that there was a problem to begin with.

None of us know what life has in store for us, and I believe that life is a sequence of events that become linked by what we make of them. I am a great believer in things happening for a reason and that everything we do—coupled with what others do to or with us—affects and guides us through our life journey. My life has always been very difficult, to the point that as a young man growing up Catholic I questioned God's reasoning daily. I have, however, tried to learn from every single experience, and I have developed a way of seeing my own life as being all about timing. If things happen for a reason, then we just have to wait sometimes to see what that reason was.

I look at everything as character building and path forming. If someone had told me ten years ago that I would be doing the job I now have and writing a book about my life, I would have thought they were mad. I spent my childhood learning the hard way about the consequences of domestic violence and child abuse, and the effect this can have on young people and children living in these environments. I was not at the same point educationally as my peers when the system wanted to judge me, and so my self-esteem was always quite low until very recently.

When my teachers wanted me to concentrate on math or English, I was wondering whether social services was going to pick us up from school that day because we had not seen our mum that morning (and this normally meant that she was unrecognizable or unable to move). By the time I was seven years old, this was an ordinary occurrence in our lives. Violence was to always play a big part in my life and was something that I would struggle to control in myself until very recently. To this day, I am still haunted by some images and memories from my childhood and from my own adult life, and I am hoping that writing this book will help put some of these memories to rest.

Timing is relevant, because by acknowledging that I was unable to learn effectively as a child, it gave me the drive to want another chance, to prove that I was more capable than many teachers and headmistresses had made me feel. I was judged at an inappropriate age, and I have come to feel that it is unfair that all children in this country (the UK) are judged the same regardless of the sometimes obvious disadvantages that some children and young people have to contend with. How can someone who has no wish to even have a future know what he is meant to want to do with it when it arrives? How have people not seen that the reason lots of teenagers who are disadvantaged drop out of education in the last year do so as a defense mechanism?

To suddenly realize that the one thing that has kept you safe and sane over the past eleven years (meaning school) is going to be gone is a nightmare, and the thought of fifty years or more living the life you already hate is just unbearable for some. Many are forced to turn to a life of alcohol and drugs to even attempt to do this.

I was expected to fail by just about every adult I had met, and they were quite happy to tell me what a parasite they thought I was going to be. I knew deep down that it was unfair because it was not me they were judging, but that their opinions were mostly based on my parents or siblings. At least in my day, it was purely a class thing; now it is much worse, as the pressure on teachers to achieve has led to a labeling culture that forces young people into a similar situation to my own in the EBD system (emotional and behavioral difficulties).

I was not able to concentrate in school, and we did not have the money for school meals or PE kits. I was never given the money for school trips, and I was constantly trying to hide the marks on me so that I would not be taken away from my mum. So maybe I was a little distracted, maybe I was a bit of a loner, maybe I did need attention when others did not. I think it is sad that I (and many others) have been judged on this. We should not be written off as unteachable by those who have had the opportunity to help us.

I have really enjoyed learning over the past five years, and I have achieved amazing things. I am reaching the highest academic levels and doing so at an Ivy League university. I am sort of happy now in life, and I gave up worrying about people who do not even worry about themselves a long time ago. My wife and children have watched me, not only overcome great personal tragedy and go on to do great things for young people in the same situation as I was, but also to find out lots of things about myself.

I have come to realize that I am a good learner and a good student, and now I always strive to get high marks in everything I do. I want to help young people who read this to understand that who you are at sixteen is not the same person you will be at twenty-five or indeed thirty-five, and that everybody gets their chance to shine. The trick is to never stop looking for opportunities and to know that it is the system that is judging you at sixteen that has the problem, not yourselves.

EARLY MEMORIES

I DO NOT know much about my early childhood, as I think a lot of it was deliberately blocked out. However, I will write the bits I know or think I remember, and hopefully memories will come flooding back. I must mention as well that this will be a journey into the unknown for me. I am really apprehensive about doing this project (as I will call it). I do not wish to dwell on bad memories or to relive my past unnecessarily, but for the sake of understanding, I feel I must try.

I know that I was born in Newry, County Down, in Northern Ireland in 1972 and that I was the third son of three boys and later a girl. I will not name my siblings, as I do not feel it would be fair to them, since they experienced our childhoods rather differently than I did. My family was Irish Catholic, and so religion was a big part of our lives growing up, although I am probably more of an atheist now (but I do still find myself saying prayers now and then, especially when children are in hospital or, worse, missing on the news). I will not pretend to know much about this time, as I was still a baby, but for the sake of clarity, I will give as much detail as I have managed to uncover for myself.

My mother came from a large family as did my father, some of whom I have managed to meet over the years and some of whom we were not allowed to meet for whatever reason. My mum's family was very close, and all married and remained in Newry, although I believe that some of my cousins have ventured farther afield. My father's family all seem to live on one estate in Newry—most even on one street. Both families were very big drinkers, and this was also to become a big part of our lives.

As I said, I was born in Newry in 1972, and I was baptized within twenty-four hours into the Catholic church. My mum lived in a small house not far from the rest of her family—her parent's house was just 200 yards or so away. My mum had gone directly against her father's wishes in being with my dad, as my mum's father hated mine with a vengeance. This was to have a huge bearing on my mum's life, as he died when we were young and my mum always felt that the rest of the family had blamed her as a contributing cause.

Anyway, my dad was heavily involved with the wrong people in Northern Ireland at the time, and so he was away from home a lot. My mum said that he had to remain on the run in the south of the country most of the time, although he did slip over the border to see us from time to time. It was this connection that led us to England. My dad, by all accounts, was sent to rob something in the south of Ireland, but Dad being Dad, he decided to keep the money and flee to England. My mum was completely unaware of all of this until she received word from my dad that he was waiting for her in England. He had blown all the money and been captured by the police in England for the robbery.

I think I was about three years old when my mum put us all on the Belfast-to-Liverpool ferry for the first time to meet him in England, and

I suppose that this is where this story really begins. My mum was leaving everything she knew behind to follow what I think she must have felt was the right and Catholic thing to do: support her husband through thick and thin. From what I have managed to figure out, we were moved straight to Somerset and put in a caravan (mobile home) until a house could be found. My dad made a lot of lifelong acquaintances on this site, ones who would inevitably lead to a life of crime and prison and, above all, violence.

My mum was shunned by her whole family for many years for this move, and because of my dad, she could never return to Newry as his wife. She was an outcast from her own town and culture because of the man she had chosen. She would live to regret this for her entire life. I think about the choices she had to make back then, and I really sympathize with her. What choice did she have, really? To stay in Ireland as a single mother for life, or to try and get a divorce? In Ireland, this would have been unheard of and certainly would have meant some form of social isolation—not to mention the fact that many of the people whom my father had upset lived and worked in Newry, and so living in Newry would have been a nightmare.

I do not think my mum knew exactly what had happened until she landed in the UK, and by then it would have been nearly impossible to return. She decided to stand by him and try and make a new life in England for the sake of us boys, and soon she was pregnant with my little sister. My dad was full of big ideas for our new future in Somerset, and my mum was still young enough to believe him.

I know that my mum suffered many years of physical and mental abuse from my dad, and I think it would be easy for him to blame the change in circumstances for this, but unfortunately I have discovered that the one reason my mother's dad hated him so much was the beatings she took from him whilst they were still courting. I mention this here because my young life is just one big domestic incident to me, and I wanted you to understand that the things he did were not because of the incident in Ireland but rather a personality trait that was always visible to everyone else but my mum. Maybe she felt that it was the troubles he was involved in growing up that triggered his anger and that moving away from the mess would change him. Whatever she thought, it was obvious to everyone else that he was a nasty piece of work.

We were all very young at this point, although I think my eldest brother remembers more than the rest of us about this time. He has told us about the fun we had on the farms around the site, and apparently, we had some good friends at the time. I can sort of remember playing hide-and-seek in a barn once, but as with much of my young life, it is all a little blurry.

We lived on the caravan site in Wellington for about nine months before we were offered a house in Taunton. This was to be my home until I was eleven. The house was quite big as far as council properties go—it was a four bedroom house with a great big garden around the back. I shared a room with my brother for most of that time, except when my eldest brother went into care much later. I don't remember much about the neighbors except that everyone was terrified of my dad. He was a big man by anybody's standards, with red hair and the temper to match.

They were mostly elderly neighbors, and most tried to befriend and help my mum in the beginning, but my father was so unpredictably violent that they eventually just avoided eye contact altogether. My mum was a stunningly beautiful woman, and I think this was a major problem with regards to my dad. He was so jealous and paranoid (which tends to be a trait in most women beaters I have met), maybe because he knew what a horrible man/husband/dad he really was. But it is unfortunately more likely that he convinced himself that she was flirting and driving him to it. My eldest brother seems to share many of these traits when it comes to women, especially the pretty ones—although I must say that it took a lot of counseling and therapy before I myself was completely free. I have had my moments of domestic horribleness, and I am sure my wife Lisa could share a few stories of her own.

I had serious attachment issues, and Lisa and I have had to work hard to remain together. I will discuss this more as the story progresses, but I wanted to be honest and not make it seem like I came out unscathed. Lisa and I both came into this relationship with serious baggage to work through, but we have supported each other in doing this and I think we have managed to succeed against all the odds, both in marriage and as parents. I really do owe her my life, because if she hadn't given me a purpose in life all those years ago, I almost certainly would have died very young.

My young life was what most would call extremely abusive. I was subjected to all types of cruelties, and some of which I will not be able to share publicly. I am not writing this book to get at anybody or to try and make myself feel better, but more to help anyone else living a similar life to remain focused and hopeful for their own futures.

I was a very emotional child and not the kind of son my father wanted. I was fussy when it came to food, and I was very scared of life in general.

I was always made to feel different or inadequate in some way because of these character traits, and so I was always an easy target. My father told me once how he had hated me "from the minute I was born," and I think my siblings picked up on this. And so, even to me, I was the problem. Having a stammer later on didn't help much either.

I was always an honest child, and this was to be another downfall of mine. I loved my mum and I knew she loved me, and we tried to look out for each other. My mum would cook me separate meals when she could, and I tried to eat them quickly so as not to get caught. She was under strict orders that I had to eat the same as everyone else, and she would get in real trouble if she was found cooking different food for me. This was a living nightmare for me, as I was having the same trouble with the nuns at my primary school where the headmistress (whom I will not name and shame, although she was probably, next to my dad, the most evil and sadistic person I have ever met would make me sit in the dining hall all day sometimes if I refused to eat.

I can remember once we were out "trick-or-treating" when I was about six or seven when we all saw my dad naked in another woman's house. My brothers told me not say anything to my mum, but I was so upset I had to tell her. Of course, back then I did not know that my brothers were trying to protect my mum from a beating, and so again it would have seemed to them like I was the problem. Let's face it: if I had kept my mouth shut, then my mum would never have known and might not have been beaten up, and I would not have had the beating I received to make me say that I hadn't see him.

But if I am honest, I would still tell her today. I do not know why, but I see that as a good quality now. She deserved to know, and he needed to know that I was not that scared of him. I like to think that is why he hated me so much—maybe I scared him.

It was really hard because I did not know why my brothers did not back me up, as they had seen it, too. And why were they not upset about what they had seen? Since they were denying things, it made it easy for my dad to accuse me of being a little troublemaker and beat a denial out of me. I can see things differently at the moment, but I think that I still carry a lot of the anger from these injustices with me and it has definitely had an impact on my life—however, not as bad an impact as the one lying to protect him had on my brothers, who unfortunately have gone on to share many of his traits when it comes to their own partners and unfortunately their children.

I was a little too soft for my family. I tried to be as hard as the others, but it always seemed to backfire on me in some way. If I tried to stand up for myself, I was always in the wrong, and when I attempted to join in play fighting, I always ended up in tears. This infuriated my dad, and he made a point of letting everyone know how disappointed he was—once even dressing me up in my sister's clothes and locking me outside of the house. This is one of the worst memories I have of my early childhood because all of my friends were outside. In fairness, some of them did not laugh; I think they could not believe it was happening.

My dad was a big drinker, and back in those days, the pubs closed at 2:30 p.m. and so it was quite common for my dad to return home drunk on a

Saturday just before the wrestling started on ITV. This became a time of dread, as he would come back and try and make us all get involved with the wrestling. I always got hurt and would be ridiculed, even by my little sister, who my dad would allow to hurt me for the others' entertainment. My dad would hold me down and get my brothers to give me dead arms and legs by punching me continuously. I would try and take it to prove I could, but I would always end up in tears. My mum would try and stop it but would just risk trouble for herself, and if she knew he was going back out, then this was never worth it.

I think my siblings got used to using me as a vent for a lot of their own confusions. We were all witnessing some seriously violent behavior, and none of us were being spoken to about it. My mum tried her best to keep things behind closed doors like you did back then, and we did not want to cause any more trouble. It was at about four or five years old that the violence took another twist for me. He would beat my mum weekly and sometimes daily—and I mean beat her. He would treat her like a man his size, and he could launch her across the room with one blow.

My dad would come home from the pub already having planned exactly what level of abuse he was going to dish out. I learned this young, as the arguments were already decided by the time he came home. My mum would try and cover every base just in case he was in a nasty mood. At one point, she tried to be asleep when he came home, but he would just wake her up when he came in. Soon enough, he made it quite obvious to me that this was also aimed at me. He would come into my room at night, grab me (still sleeping), and drag me downstairs to watch while he shouted at and beat my mum.

This went on for all of my young life and led to a lot of my sleeping issues later on. I would have to block out the screaming somehow, so I would shake my head uncontrollably and make weird and abnormal noises to drown it out. This led to years of bullying at home and serious problems when I was in care. I could not stop doing it as I got older and I would do it in my sleep as well. My brothers would use it to wind me up, and kids in children's homes refused to share a room with me because I was so noisy. I have even had to explain to my own kids why it happens, because if I dream about my dad it still happens to this day, much to my disappointment.

My kids understand, I think, but for years I simply avoided sleep to prevent people from hearing me and also to prevent the dreams that the years of being awoken to extreme violence had led to. I have tried to get help with this over the years, but some things, I am afraid, are too inbuilt to change, and I have accepted that my sleeping issues are for life. I try and live my life in a way that will hopefully lead to enough good memories to cancel out the bad ones, and hopefully, one day my dreams will be of good times.

I think the worst incident was one particular Christmas—I would have been about six or seven at the time. I had spent hours trying to stay awake for Santa (as we all do at that age). I must have fallen asleep, because the next thing I knew, I was bouncing off the wall in the front room. I was half asleep still and terrified. My dad was shouting at my mum that she was a whore or something similar. I had to watch him pull what I think was a child's pram from under the Christmas tree and proceed to beat my mum what seemed like a hundred times with it.

She was battered and needed hospital treatment. I got up and tried to stop him, but he simply gave me a backhander and I fell in the corner crying. I wanted to run out of the room, but I could not take my eyes of my mum, who I could see was going to die any minute if he did not stop. I was so scared for my mum; she was the only person I knew whom I loved back then and who loved me. I think I shut down at some point, because I do not know who called an ambulance or got help. But someone must have heard the screams, because I woke up Christmas morning and she was not there. I thought he had killed her, and I cried until someone told me she was in hospital but we could not see her.

It was probably the worst Christmas ever. My brothers blamed me for the whole thing, saying that I must have been awake when he came home and started it. When I look back now, they must have been trying to figure out my role in it all for themselves. Why was I the only one who ever saw anything? Why did he choose me to watch? And why didn't I help Mum? Perhaps they felt it should have been me, because I was the only common denominator other than my mum and dad.

My mum was hospitalized for a few days, and a family friend stepped in to help. Dad simply went to the pub and avoided eye contact with us for a few days until, in his wisdom, we would have all forgiven him. By now I hated him so much it hurt. I was terrified of him and he knew it. He would sit next to me and make sudden movements so that I would jump and he could make the others laugh at me. He had started getting angry that I was developing a stutter as well (maybe he felt responsible), and I was punished badly if I stuttered when speaking to him.

The older I got, the more the stammer became a big problem. My brothers and sister figured out that they could use it well to get me into trouble. And if I was trying to say that one of them had done something to me, they could finish my sentences for me, which as you can imagine meant that I was continuously frustrated and felt unlistened to. As I said earlier, I think a lot of these issues stayed with me for many years before I was able to let the anger and resentment go. I realized eventually that I was the only one who cared and so carrying the negative feelings around were hurting no one but myself.

My dad was so cruel that I can understand how difficult it might be to comprehend. I am still trying to understand it all myself. It was not only violence at home we were witnessing, though; we were learning quickly that my dad was a local hard man and we knew how to use this to our advantage. We would get our dad involved in our arguments in the street (which he loved). When I look back on it now, I could cry, honestly. I can remember my brothers making me say that a neighbor had spat at me so that my dad would have a go, but it went horribly wrong and my dad beat this poor man half to death. My brothers thought this was really funny, but even at that young age I knew it was wrong and I felt seriously ashamed—which was to be a common feeling over the coming years.

Although I can talk now about feelings of shame and disgust, at the time I was busy trying to survive so I kept a lot of these feelings to myself, believing the feelings themselves to be my problem. That was why dad didn't like me—it was because I was too soft, not a Shorthall, a weakling! I battled with this my whole young life right into adulthood, trying to decide which person I was meant to be: the horrible Shorthall I had learned to be or the decent young man trapped inside a criminal past (I know how much of a cliché that must sound, but I do not know how else to say it). It was hard because a bit of me just wanted him to accept me, and I believed that the only way this could happen would be by my proving myself criminally or violently. I regret so much those wasted years, but like I will soon explain, it was all part of the rich tapestry that is my life and it was all "character building stuff."

We did have friends to grow up with, and I still see many around town. The funny thing is, most are still down there in Taunton's equivalent to the Bronx in New York, and their kids seem to be living much the same lives as we did. This is not a criticism but simply an observation, and I know that I am still not that far from it myself. But that particular area of my hometown is very depraved, and unfortunately, I know that kids are judged in society just for living down there—I have heard it firsthand several times. I have heard people in offices arguing about who has to go down there like it is a quarantined area or something. I don't want to dwell on this, as I am no sociologist, but I think it is sad that we still live in a society where you are judged and categorized based on your post code.

I witnessed several extremely violent episodes in my younger years. A particularly bad one was the taxi incident. An Irish man had shown up at the house to drop some money off to my mum that he owed to my dad, but the money was short and an argument broke out. Unfortunately for the man, my dad arrived home from the pub as this was ending and the man was calling my mum something unpleasant. The man tried to get away, but my dad had arrived home in a taxi and had made the taxi block his car in. It was horrific. We watched my dad put his arm through the side window of the man's car and half drag the man out. Before he could talk, my dad had head-butted him directly in the face, splitting his whole face wide open. He did this several times, and then with the man semiconscious, he pulled him out of the car and began to stamp all over him. This was in the middle of a Saturday afternoon with an audience of maybe twenty young children.

The amazing thing was, no one must have said anything to the police, as my dad was not even arrested. He went on the run that day, thinking they would be looking for him, but they never came so he was back within a few days. This was when we first noticed that our friends suddenly weren't allowed out to play or we were only allowed to play in their gardens. I can understand this now; as a parent, we all want to protect our kids. But from a child's perspective, it was just more isolation for no apparent reason, so again I just thought that it must have been me or indeed us.

Another memorable incident was when my Uncle Jimmy, my mum's brother, came to visit from Ireland. I have never managed to find out exactly what happened, but from what I can gather, my dad actually accused my mum of having a relationship with her own brother. I woke in the middle of the night as my door came off its hinges and my dad landed on top of my uncle in the middle of my bedroom floor. It was awful. My mum was screaming for my dad to get off, but he had his thumbs dug right into Jimmy's eyes and there was blood running down the side of Jimmy's face as Dad was beating his head against the floor.

My uncle tried to fight back, but he was tiny compared to my dad. My dad mutilated him. He did his trademark stamping all over his head. My room never had a door again after that night, and unfortunately, mum's brother has never really spoken to her since. My dad was unrepentant as usual and life just continued. I hated being in that room, though, and begged my brothers to let me have a room with a door, but they thought it was funny that I was scared and so they said no. I needed a door because sometimes that was my only warning he was coming.

My dad was extremely criminally active by this time, and we always had a variety of people around the house selling all kinds of goodies. My dad always seemed to have plenty of money and violence was never far away, whether it was my dad taking people home from the pub and then turning on them or someone showing up trying to get money out of my dad, which always ended in violence. My dad told me years later that "violence was cheaper"!

Mum tried to give us as normal a life as possible, and dad did go to jail sometimes for a couple of months here and there, but these periods were always over before you got to enjoy them. My mum would make us go to church on Sunday and she tried to get us equipped for school. The problem she had was that my dad was bringing us up to be little crooks, to "rob the English." He was even telling us to rob our teachers' purses! I tried to like school, but it was not easy, as I will soon explain. I hated going to church, even Sunday school, purely because we always felt watched all the time, as if we were little thieves or something!

You may have found my earlier comment about my primary school headmistress a little harsh, so I will justify my reasons. When we arrived from Ireland, my mum found a Catholic school she wanted to send us to. Thinking that they would be sympathetic to our needs, she made the mistake of telling the school what my dad was and all about our situation. Sister shared this information with anyone and everyone, to the point that even a couple of years ago when in a local doctor's surgery my name appeared on the board, and my wife then heard an elderly person who sat in front of us tell her friend all about the infamous Shorthalls and what a curse on the school we had been.

Back then, we were often collected from school by the police or social services because my dad had hospitalized my mum and we had to go into care. Sister took great pleasure in doing this as publicly as possible. We would often arrive at school with bad bruising and clear marks of child abuse, which she must have chosen to ignore. Instead, she would make me sit in the main hall all afternoon until I ate food that was making me physically ill. She let the rest of my peers vote on whether I should be allowed to stay in their class, and when they voted no, I was taught by just her and my desk was in the main school entrance for everyone to see.

In my opinion, she was the nastiest person I had ever met, because to me she was supposed to care. I know she did not, because I can clearly remember those who did. Knowing what we all know now about the Catholic church's attitude toward child abuse, I suppose this should come as little surprise. Some of our teachers even tried to get something done for us, but Sister always put a stop to it. I can remember a certain classroom assistant called Mrs. Windsor who had offered to pay for me to go on a school trip (as my parents never did), and Sister said that I could not go as it was unfair to those parents who did pay.

I could go on with a hundred stories about Sister, but that is not the purpose of this book. I just wanted to explain that where we should have felt safe and secure, we were made to feel unworthy and were stigmatized deliberately and for no apparent good reason other than one person's personal prejudiced feelings. School was always going to be difficult, as I was coming after my two older brothers who, let's just say, were no angels. We were skipping school by the time I was eight, and we were also quite good shoplifters by this time. I do not want that to sound like a skill; it is simply the truth. We would stop at every shop on the way to school and steal something, either sweets or pens and pencils.

I was once made—well, let's say "encouraged"—to steal a purse from my favorite teacher at primary school. She was what we would now call the reception class teacher, and she was lovely. My brothers made me sneak into her classroom and steal it from her handbag. I hid it in the bushes outside of her classroom until the end of the school day, but thankfully I was seen and we were caught when we tried to retrieve it. I was so ashamed: the whole school knew what I had done and I felt like they were all talking about me, which, let's face it, they probably were and rightfully so.

My mum went mental as usual, and my dad gave us all a good hiding, but this time on my mum's orders. When we were still little and he beat us all, which he did do sometimes. He would use a belt, and it was pretty random which end he used. If he was pissed off in any way, it would be the buckle end, but if he was feeling all right, it would just be the belt folded in half. He would beat us into a corner somewhere, where the luckiest kid was the one at the bottom, whereas the ones at the top got the worst of it.

I have just remembered a very odd story but a very relevant memory. It was a time when he completely threw us all by "pretending" to beat us. We were all upstairs waiting for him to come home on the promise from my mum of a good hiding. I can't remember what we had done, but he came home from the pub in a really good mood, only to be ranted at by my mum and told to give us all a beating. He came upstairs, and we were all cowering in the corner, waiting as usual. He took off his belt, but instead of hitting us he started hitting the wall with his belt and whispering to us to pretend to scream, which of course we did willingly. This may sound like a great story and you would think that we would be grateful; however, what it actually did was give us all false hope. Every time we were expecting any kind of beating, we all hoped right up to the first swing of his arm that he was going to hit the wall, but he never did again.

It was confusing growing up in our house. When it came to crime, we were encouraged to steal by my dad at any opportunity. He would make me put things in my pocket in shops, and he would think nothing of stopping the car and making us jump out and grab stuff from gardens or wherever. The confusion was the reaction when we got caught. I could understand my parents being angry in front of the police and other agencies, but in reality they should not have been punishing us for it when they were teaching it! I can remember being arrested once with my brothers for stealing a pen, and we were taken to the police station (bear in mind that I was no more than ten years old). My mum arrived at the station and proceeded to beat me around the head—the police allowed her to do this!—telling me to tell the truth and calling me every name under the sun. I wanting the beating to stop, so I told the police exactly what had happened and I was then released, only to be beaten all the way home for "grassing" my brothers up!

I unfortunately would require these early shoplifting skills to survive later in life, but when I was a child, it was one of my biggest embarrassments. We were always watched everywhere we went, even in people's houses (which to me was horrible, because I would never have stolen from someone's house). At primary school, we were never given any positions of trust, not even altar boy for the church, which I always wanted to do. It's funny, but when I look back, we were never picked for anything: not school plays, church readings, or even to take the register back.

By the time I was in my last year at the school, I was not even in a class. As I said earlier, my desk was in the main entrance and my teacher was the headmistress. It was horrible. I was the first thing that anyone who visited the school saw, and I was forever being asked what I had done that was so naughty that I sat where I was. And the truth was, I did not know. I think it was because of my refusing to eat the school meals and thus always being late back after lunch. It was decided that I was just being obstructive and I should not be allowed to disrupt the rest of the class, or something like that. I asked my mum to come to the school to see the headmistress, but it never happened, and before you knew it, I was leaving to go to secondary school.

I do have some good early memories, and one was when my dad was in prison (a period in my life which I will go into in a bit). Social services organized and paid for it (I think), but it was a good memory all the same. We went to Lyme Regis in Devon; we were in a flat on a second floor, and we had views of the park and the sea. We could not believe it was real. My mum looked happier than I had ever seen her, and I can remember thinking how nice it was without dad, but I dared not say it. My brothers and sister missed him and would talk about him every day; they could not wait to tell the other kids that our dad was in jail (like it was a cool thing?). They wrote to him every night and then made me, saying that it would cause arguments if I didn't. I would write the same stuff every time and he must have known—that's if he even read mine. I wish I had been clever enough to test him by writing something that I really thought, but it's just as well I didn't, as with my luck, that would have been the one letter he did read.

I remember something else about that holiday that I am sure my mum will not mind me mentioning. We (the boys) were all involved in an incident in the park opposite the flat, and a local police officer escorted us back. The officer knocked on the door and it was open, so we told him to go on in, which he did only to find my mum lying topless on the balcony. He was only a young officer, and he was completely flustered—it was hilarious. I can remember noticing how my mum looked different. I am not sure how to explain it, but she looked young, pretty, and I suppose normal.

Social services did have a lot to do with my family while I was growing up, and we were continuously in and out of local authority care and foster placements. Some were quite good, but we never really enjoyed our respite because if we were in care then it meant our mother was in hospital or at home being battered. It has always fascinated me that social workers thought there was any benefit to removing us after the fact; surely if we already knew what had happened, then removing us made us feel even more insecure. I personally just needed to know that my mum was all right, but nobody would even discuss this with us and would simply tell us to try not to worry and to let the grown-ups worry about it.

Every now and then we would get visitors from Ireland, but this was normally just one big drinking session, a fight or two, and then a week or two of my mum hating England and my dad hating everybody. We were never seen as children by my mum's family, just "his" kids, and again, we felt it. One good thing about them all drinking was that it was an opportunity for us to make some money, singing Irish rebel songs for them or taking part in races around the block that they would all bet on (not knowing or even considering that my dad was controlling the whole thing). We could sometimes earn £10 each, which was a lot of money in those days.

The drinking even created some very funny stories. For instance, I can remember my dad coming home one summer afternoon and trying to fall asleep in his chair. My mum had other ideas and started nagging him to cut the hedge in the front garden like he had promised earlier. He tried pretending he was asleep and ignoring her, but she was having none of it. Eventually, he leapt out of his seat and we all thought he was about to hit her, but instead he went straight out the front of the house and got into his car.

He reversed out of the driveway and then got out, leaving the car parked in the middle of the street while he started hunting around in the boot for something. What he emerged with was a long length of rope and a chain, which he then proceeded to tie around the hedge in different places and attached to the tow bar on his car. What he did next was hilarious, as my mum had not seen any of this preparation. My dad got into the car and drove off at high speed up the road, tearing the hedge, roots and all, right out of the ground. You must bear in mind that the hedge was about six feet high and was almost blocking out the sun from the front of the house. We had never been able to see the houses across the street from the front room before, and so when my mum walked in from the kitchen to see daylight, she dropped what she was holding. My dad simply parked the car back in the drive and told us to clear up the mess whilst he went back to his chair for a sleep.

I had some good friends back then, and some of them witnessed some horrific things and still stood by me. My father never cared who was around when he was fighting or doing dodgy deals. Other parents knew exactly what he was doing, and so some of my friends were banned from playing with me. I sometimes had to get other young people to call for my friends for me so that their parents would not see me. It always felt like I was dirty or something. My friends were always telling me to hide because their parent's car was coming or their sister was in the park. It was horrible, if I am honest, and it left me feeling inadequate for a long time in my adult life. I was lucky enough to do some work with a great psychologist a couple of years ago who helped me with this immensely.

And then, suddenly, I had a life-changing moment. We awoke one morning when I was about nine or ten years old to the police banging the door down and then proceeding to drag my dad out of bed and down the stairs. It was awful. My dad must have known that he was in big trouble because he fought like I had never seen him fight before. It took all of eight policemen to restrain him in the end, and he ended up hospitalizing several during the raid. I can remember him punching one so hard that the man went through the front door and straight through our garden fence into the road, and I promise that this is no exaggeration.

It was chaos for about an hour, but by then my dad had been removed to the cells and my mum was busy "helping the police with their inquiries." It was amazing, really. We had no idea that my dad had been heading up a military-style burglary team and our house was full of the stuff. The police began removing big grandfather clocks and boxes of silver out of our lofts and sheds until there was a van full of these items. I did not know at this point that this was going to lead to probably the most important and influential time of my young years. It turned out that there had been several arrests all over the estate, and there would be several kids without a father for some years and even one without a mother.

My dad was remanded into custody, and just like that we were a single parent family. I loved it. And this leads nicely into the next chapter of my life.

We were still the local scum to everyone else and we still had no money or nice things, but to me being fatherless gave us a chance to live normal lives, to do things like a family. This never really happened how I imagined it would, as my mum had began drinking as much as he did before he went away and she always had a hangover. But the violence had stopped for a while (in our house, anyway) and that was enough to make life more livable at least. We even got on quite well as brothers and sister for the only time I can remember in my young life.

One good memory I do have of my childhood that I have only remembered recently was of a summer when the youth service or somebody similar built a play area on some waste ground at the end of our street. We lived in the most depraved part of town, and we only had one park within walking distance that was full of glue sniffers most days. Glue sniffing and solvent abuse was quite fashionable back then—luckily enough, I was still too young to be interested in drugs or it would have been easy. Our streets were lined with glue bags and empty gas cans, but I suppose that was better than it is now. Unfortunately as times have changed so have the fashions, and now they are more interested in heroin and crack, and different things line the streets.

Anyway, back to my good memory. The play area was only there for the summer, as they were building bungalows on the land in the autumn, but it was amazing while it lasted. They built swings and climbing frames and, best of all, a zip line, which none of us had ever seen before in real life. We were there from 8:00 a.m. until 8:00 p.m., and so was every other kid on the estate. They had workers there all day, and so there wasn't much fighting or you were banned from the site and they came to see you at home. The zip line lasted probably ten seconds if that, but it felt like flying. I would queue up over and over again until I was called home every day for the first week before I got tired of it. And after that, one of my best friends—a lad called Anthony—and I would sit on top of the climbing frame watching everyone else pull funny faces whilst coming down the slide.

The scheme ended up over running slightly, as the building must have been delayed or something and it was still there I think on bonfire night. It was amazing: they dismantled everything on the site, and as it was all wood, it was all used to build a massive fire in the middle and everyone was asked to bring some food for a barbeque. We only had potatoes to take, but they were gratefully received, wrapped in tinfoil, and placed in a safe that was sitting just inside the fire. I can remember wondering what the youth worker was doing at first, but he told me to be patient and I would see. I didn't eat anything else all night waiting to see what the potato would look like when it came out. I am not sure what I was expecting, but what I got was my first ever jacket potato. Maybe that was exotic food in my house, as the thought of cooking potatoes in anything other than fat or oil was, I think, sacrilege in Ireland. I was given a big lump of butter with it, and it was the most amazing thing I had ever eaten. I think I bugged my mum about it constantly for a month before she tried them herself, but to be honest, I have never had a jacket potato that tasted anything near as good as that first one I had at the end of my road over thirty years ago.

Northern Ireland

I WAS LOOKING forward to leaving primary school, as I hoped that the stigma would end at a bigger school—but I was not allowing for the fact that my two older brothers had been before me. But life at home was still much better, as my dad was still in prison. When it came to his sentencing, he got five and a half years and was sent to Shepton Mallet Prison. There were good times for me for a while. We were very poor, like I said, and we felt it, but my mum was well in with all the local thieves, so we normally got decent stuff for birthdays or Christmases. But then a friend of my dad, Chris, moved in as a lodger at my dad's request, and this was to mean another big turning point in my young life.

He was a really nice man, and he soon took a liking to my mum, who I must say was still a stunning woman despite the years of beatings from my dad. I was unaware of all of this until a fight broke out between Chris and my eldest brother. My brother had spoken to my dad on a prison visit and my dad told him to keep an eye on things, so he snuck outside one night and caught my mum and the lodger kissing. All hell broke loose, and my brother called my mum some horrible names. I was surprised obviously, but I liked the man and I knew he would never hurt us, so I was quite excited. Unfortunately, my eldest brother refused to live with my mum anymore and was placed into local authority care. I should say that this was also due to his continued offending behavior and truanting, which was getting out of control.

My mum decided that she wanted to leave my dad and it was time to tell him. She did try the "Dear John" route, but he was having none of it, and so she arranged a visit with his probation officer and some extra prison officers so that she could talk to him face to face. This was a disaster, and he managed to get hold of my mum and break her cheekbone and fracture her skull. She was beat to a pulp, and we were taken straight into care. We did not see her for about eight weeks, and her face was still unrecognizable then. It broke my heart to see her like that, and I ran away. I can remember being coaxed back inside to see her by carers, but I couldn't look at her like that—it didn't even look like my mum. It had been weeks and she was still unrecognizable. I was kept in care for quite a while longer until my mum was completely recovered and I was happy; if I never saw her look like that again, I would have been even happier, but that was not going to be.

Chris was still seeing my mum, although he was away working a lot of the time. Mum decided that she wanted to return to Ireland, and he was willing to come with us if my mum wanted it. This was brilliant news as far as I was concerned: a new start with a new dad. How wrong would I be! I had started secondary school by then and had been there for about six months. It was not going well and so the timing seemed perfect.

My mum had to get in touch with her family to find out whether she could return safely, and she was told that she was welcome to return with us and the lodger but that dad would be killed if he came back. Within the next six months, we were living in a caravan in a small town called Warren-point just outside Newry in County Down.

I can remember that it was my secondary school fete the Friday before we were leaving, and my brother and I were given a stall to run, charging people 20 pence or something to throw wet sponges at either the headmaster or some of the teachers. It was brilliant because we were right opposite the mini motorbike track, which was, I think, £1 a go. Every time we made enough money for a go on the bikes, we were gone. We had a great laugh and we even took all our friends to a local under-sixteen disco in a pub afterward with what money was leftover. I know it was stealing and I am not condoning it, but we didn't know any better and we were leaving town for what we thought was going to be forever.

It was not such a good time for my mum, though, as my eldest brother was refusing to move to Ireland and was making her chose between Chris and him. It was not fair, really, but he thought he was doing the right thing by my dad, which I can understand now. It was never going to be a choice really, because my mum had already made her mind up that we were going to Ireland, and so my brother was to stay in care in England until my dad was released.

I think a bit of me thought we were going home and that we would finally feel welcome somewhere. I am not sure how to explain it, but I think it felt like it was the beginning of my proper life, the one I had always been wishing for. I never really felt as though we belonged in Taunton or were even wanted there. I was convinced that Ireland would feel like home and we would all live happily ever after.

We were soon given a home in Northern Ireland by the local council: a small four-bedroom house in Warren-point, County Down. It was a nice house and it backed onto the town park, which was very convenient for walking the dog. (Chris had bought me a dog that I called Rambo. It was a Chow Chow, so the name probably wasn't that appropriate, but I loved him dearly). The one thing I really remember about this house was that the bathroom was downstairs and the house was always freezing cold in the mornings. We would fight over old plastic lemonade bottles just to use them as hot water bottles. They were lethal really and a nightmare in the mornings when they were cold.

We lived right at the bottom of the Mourne Mountains, and everything was still coal heated. I can remember lying in bed on cold winter mornings waiting with dread to hear who my mother was going to pick on to get up and light the fire. At the time, we thought it was the worst punishment in the world.

Mum and Chris were to be married when he joined us in Ireland, but he was working in America while we got settled. Ireland was not quite as good as I had hoped. I had not considered the fact that we would be going to Irish Catholic schools with British accents and a divorced mum. The second bit about the divorced mum would probably seem insignificant to most people, but it did cause us a lot of problems. We were hated at school; both my brother and I (who was just two years older than me) had a really hard time. We had to fight together every day. We had made a pact after the first few weeks that if they hit one of us, they had to hit us both.

This was a useful pact in regards to bringing me and my brother closer, and we shared probably the best few years together we have ever had. We did manage to make some proper friends by the second year, and things began to settle down on that front. The next problem was my mum's remarriage to Chris. I made the mistake of saying at school that this was happening, and suddenly everyone was saying that my mum must be some kind of slag for having two husbands—that is how absurd religious communities can be.

It took a long time, but things did eventually settle down and, like I said, we made some friends. I met a lad called Booboo (nickname obviously) who was great fun and whom I had some great laughs with. I also made friends with a lad named Ronan who was the hardest kid in our year, if I remember rightly. I also met my first girlfriend, whom I shall never forget—my eldest daughter even has her name as her middle name. I will not say her name obviously, but I owe this girl a lot. She was the first person in Ireland to be nice to me and she was truly beautiful. Her dad was a doctor, I think, and she lived in a lovely house by my school. I was stupid enough to upset her one day whilst trying to impress some lads, and I have regretted it ever since. We were going out up until then, and she was the first girl I ever kissed and I think loved, but she never forgave me and we didn't speak for a long time. I would love to see her again before I die, if only to apologize for that stupid day.

As always, violence was never too far away. We lived in Northern Ireland during the troubles, and so everyone was always on edge. We were in Newry once when the PIRA (Provisional Irish Republican Army) blew up a shop called Well-Worth's at Easter time and there were eggs everywhere.

I hated going to Newry as a rule because nine times out of ten my mother would see one of her sisters, and that would mean a day in the pub. I was actually in town one day when two police officers were shot dead in front of us. It was quite surreal, really. I don't think I registered what had happened until everyone started running. I remember hearing something like fireworks going off really quickly and then a marching band started up in the high street. It turns out the band was a distraction to help the gunmen get away.

It wasn't just the adults who were capable of extreme violence, either. I was at a disco in a town called Hilltown that was about a three-mile walk into the hills from Warren-point. We were all told about a fight about to happen outside in the car park, and so we all ran out just in time to see a lad of about eighteen lift another lad up from the floor and drag his face along a barbed wire fence. It was horrific, and bits of the other lad's face were stuck on the fence for months.

My dad was still in custody through all of this, and my eldest brother had remained in care in England, although he did visit once and managed to upset most of the town by going out with the prettiest girl—a girl, I will add, whom lads had been asking out unsuccessfully for years, but she had said yes to my brother on his first try. We even got in trouble for it ourselves, with older boys giving us messages for him all the time. However, that was not the worst thing he did. He had paired up with a local lad in Newry when he had been to see my dad's family for him, and the fool had been out robbing. As you can imagine, this was not the wisest thing to do in a town controlled by the IRA. He had been burgling houses, and several people had been to Sinn Féin to report it.

In Northern Ireland back then, if you were a Catholic who became a victim of crime, you didn't go to the police; you went to the Sinn Féin office and they sorted it out themselves. The problem was that you didn't have fences in the same way we had in England that bought all the nicked gear for drugs and then sold it on. My brother and his genius mate had been selling the bits in secondhand shops, and so it was easy for the Provisionals to find out where the gear went and then just wait for them to return with more. It was a weekend when they finally came, and it was terrifying. My mum was out with her sister, and so my eldest brother was looking after us all and there was a knock on the door. My younger sister opened the door and there were three men there who asked for my brother. We innocently told them to come in, and we took them into the kitchen to see him.

My brother seemed to know instinctively that something was up because he told us to go into the front room and shut the door, which we did, but we listened at the door. They asked him to confirm who he was, and then they introduced themselves as representatives of the IRA and announced that he was to accept a punishment beating for the burglaries he had committed. They told him that all the things he had stolen had been returned to the people they belonged to and that he would need to pay back any money. It was very sudden what happened next, and although we didn't see it all, we heard plenty. Lots of noise broke out, and we could hear screaming coming from my brother. My other brother and I tried to open the door, but it was being held shut from the other side for some time. Eventually we did manage to open it, and we saw two men beating my brother with the hammer sides of hatchets (small axes). He was already badly hurt, and so when my sister started screaming, they stopped and put the hatchets away, and as quick as it had happened, they were gone.

We were all in shock, I think, and nobody spoke while we helped my brother into the front room. He was badly hurt, but he wouldn't let us get him any help. He begged us to not tell my mum what had happened until after he had returned to England in a couple of days, which we all agreed to. What he didn't know was that my mum was on her way home, as someone had been to see her to inform her of what had happened. I think she thought she might beat them to the house, but they would not have been to see her until the job was done, I am sure. It was all surface wounds, and so my brother was able to travel on time, and he left vowing to never return to Northern Ireland. I think, to be honest, my mum knew that he meant it and that it was probably for the best. He would have ended up dying over there. Between his stealing and car thefts, it was only a question of who would have killed him: the IRA for being a thief or the British army for joyriding.

The rest of us had stopped stealing things in Ireland because my mum told us the IRA would get us (they were a much better deterrent than the police), and so we behaved quite well. When Chris came back from America, we started planning the wedding and my mum seemed genuinely happy. I can remember going with him to the bank so that he could take out several thousand pounds to buy a new car with and him letting me carry the money. I felt like I had a proper dad—it was brilliant. We all had new bikes for Christmas, and my mum had a beautiful house that she was very proud of, and all was going well until I got into some serious trouble.

I was at school when someone said something about the fact that my mum would have two husbands. I did not hear exactly what was said, but I knew I had heard something. As the day went on, I found out that the lad had called my mum a whore and had said that she must love sex to have two husbands. I know now that he was just being Irish; people have no idea just how Catholic some communities are in Ireland. My mum was the only divorcée in the town, and that was bad enough, but to be getting remarried in a registry office to a Welsh Protestant was a full-on sin.

I stupidly dwelled on the comment about my mum all day, and later that evening when I saw the young lad in question, I beat him up quite badly and got arrested for assault, which unfortunately was the beginning of my own troubled youth. The RUC (Northern Ireland's police force) were really harsh, I thought. They blocked off the road with soldiers and Land Rovers and sent about twenty officers to arrest me. My mum was devastated, as she was already being talked about enough in the small town. The courts were a little bit racist as well because of my religion. I was automatically considered for a custodial sentence, which was madness—I was only thirteen years old.

I was sent to a place called St. Patrick's in Belfast for six months for the assault, and it was awful. It was run by Christian brothers who, after the nun I mentioned earlier, were the second nastiest people I had ever met—besides my dad, of course. They nicknamed me "Basil the Brit" on my arrival (due to my accent), and this name stuck throughout my stay. I was placed in a dormitory with five other lads, and my induction happened on the first night when I got what was known as my first "shoeing." This involved all the others beating me while I was asleep with their own prison-type shoes (which I can assure you are like brick, or at least were back then). I had to put up with this every night for six months.

The Christian brothers were so cruel that they would count you using punches in the arm, and one even threw me down a flight of stairs once for complaining about this. I was so afraid of them that I would not even tell my mum on the phone about the "shoe-ins" just in case they were listening to our phone calls.

I stayed at St. Pat's for the entire six months, and in a way, it did me good. Had I remained in Ireland, I doubt if I would have ever got into trouble again. Unfortunately, this was not to be. When I returned home, I found out that my dad had been released from prison and was demanding to see his children. We were told we did not have to visit if we did not want to, and so I obviously decided not to go. However, my brother and sister wanted to go and visit, and so it was arranged through social services.

My dad, however, kept them for about three months and refused to send them home—which in one way was good for me because I had the best few months of my life with my mum. I was worried that she might want to go back to England herself, but she assured me that she did not. Funny enough, at this time my mum tried to write her own story, but it was too painful, I think, and it seemed to make her drink loads more.

My brother came back to Ireland covered in tattoos and smoking dope, and this was where my association with drugs started. On top of this, my sister had not been made to go to school for months and did not want to return. Both kept on and on at my mum to speak to my dad, which she eventually did. Chris was still working in America and sending his wages back to my mum, and so living was quite good. He returned at Christmas and for holidays, but relations were strained and I could tell something was not right. My brother even stole Chris's car with some of his mates, which was directly meant to cause problems, as he later told me, since dad was telling him what to do by phone.

My brother soon found a supplier of dope in Warren-point where we were still living, and he was hanging around with kids much older than himself and I think on the fringes of political activity. He let me tag around when it suited him, and I liked the dope because it would just knock me out with no dreams—to me, this was heaven. At the same time, I had a massive hold over my brother for the first time, as my mum did not know about him smoking let alone the drugs, and so the bullying and beatings from him stopped.

Anyway, it all went pear-shaped, and soon my mum was talking to my dad regularly on the phone. I asked her again if she was going to go back, and she promised me no. But I came home from school a short time later to find that everything had been sold and we were indeed going back. My mum would not even look at me. I can remember her giving me a claw hammer and telling me to rob the gas and electric meters and then to go into town to change it up into notes (my mum was no angel, either).

We then left to get the Belfast-to-Liverpool ferry. My girlfriend didn't even get a good-bye and neither did any of my mates. Mum just wanted to leave. I don't even think she told her own brothers and sisters or her mum. I was devastated, to be honest, and I just wanted to cry, but I knew that everyone else would have turned on me if I had played it up too much. I often wonder why she didn't at least try and arrange for me to stay with one of her sisters or brothers in Ireland, as she must have known how I was feeling.

Instead, my brother and I found a way of robbing the fruit machines on the ferry and we got off the boat about a thousand pounds richer than when we got on board. And so my life of crime had started again before we even landed in England. I was worried because I was terrified of being caught again, but I thought it might at least impress my dad.

We landed in Liverpool where my dad was waiting for us. It was horrible. He did not even look at me; he just picked up and cuddled the rest of them, and then gave my mum a big squeeze, totally ignoring me. We got on the train and headed south. I sat on my own the whole way, as the tables only have four seats and there was not room for me. Deep down I knew something bad was going to happen; I was just not sure what or indeed when.

I sometimes wish we had stayed in Ireland and my mum must think the same. Her life has been a succession of upsets since her return to England, and her family has never understood why she left them a second time for more of the same. I know my mum says that she did it for us, but I think deep down it was her own hope that he had changed that took her back. We all know that we cannot choose who we fall in love with and we all hope to mold these people into the ideal visions that we hold. But I also think that she must have known that he could not change that much, as she is a clever woman, especially when it comes to people. I guess she has to live with the decisions she made, and our family is pretty fragmented as a result.

I have not spoken to my mum for a long time now, as she cannot comprehend the person I have become or the things I believe in. I wish there was a magic door that I could send all my family through to make them into better people, but something I have learned over the years tells me that they would not want to walk through the magic door anyway. My family knows the bits of them that need to change, but whether they want to change them is the issue. They think I am soft and that I am deluded about the things I am trying to do for disadvantaged young people. They like drugs, and they like the reputation that comes with being a Shorthall (although they have all taken new names except me). The difference is, I suppose, that I never did like being a Shorthall; I just wanted to be Declan and not only my father's son.

BACK IN TAUNTON

I THINK THAT all I wish to say about our return to Taunton was that it was inevitable that it would never work. We arrived in Taunton to share my dad's two-bedroom council flat in Priorswood, a predominantly working-class part of Taunton but where most liked to think they were slightly better than they actually were. Our flat was tiny by anybody's standards, and I had to share a bed in the front room with my brother whilst my little sister had a bedroom (my eldest brother was at this time living in a bedsit). This would have been quite good if it were not for the fact that I had the pleasure of waiting for my dad to return home from the pub every evening and worrying about the wake-up call in the middle of the night, but thankfully this never came—not in the same way as before, anyway.

I managed to find some old friends in and around the Priorswood area, and it was good to be the center of attention with the girls for a while. I think it was the Irish accent that did it and the fact that we still had loads of money left from the fruit machines on the boat. I was good friends with one of the lads in the close where Dad's flat was (we still see each other occasionally to this day), but my time with my family in Priorswood would be short-lived.

It was funny being back in town, and I was hoping that I would be able to start school without the labels I had endured the first time around. I was the only one thinking about school, however, as my parents didn't seem that worried about it, and so I managed to put myself straight back in the unpopular box with my siblings by asking. It was arranged that I was to begin at a school called Bishop Fox's in Taunton, and I was actually quite excited.

We lived in the flat for a while, but my dad was working on a swap with a lady who lived opposite us and only had one daughter in a three-bedroom house—and eventually, the trade took place. It was a nice house and had a massive garden and driveway. My dad hadn't really changed much, except that I noticed he was smoking lots of dope. He never smoked before we went away, but it seemed to make him laugh more, which was a good thing. It was weird being around him because you knew it was all an act. My mum was trying to act like she was glad she had come back, and my dad was trying his best to act like a different man. But the temper was still there, and it didn't take long for me to see it.

I can't remember what exactly happened, but I remember my mum telling me that I was in big trouble for something I hadn't done. In fact, it was my brother who had done it, but I couldn't say that or he would have been in the same position as me. I ran off, determined that I wasn't going to let the abuse start again, but to be honest, I was terrified. I stayed at a friend's house, and the following day we stood on the high street with some of my brother's mates when my dad's motorbike came onto the pavement and headed straight toward me (and this was a pedestrian-only area). I was about to run when a friend of my brother grabbed me; he even said sorry but that my dad had told him to do it. I was in shock—what did he mean? He had let my dad know I was there. My dad had sent them all out looking for me, and they were under strict orders to hold me if they found me.

My dad rode his bike straight into my legs and then head-butted me with his helmet still on straight in the face. I crumbled and fell over, but he made me get up and force a helmet on my face. He shouted again for me to put my helmet on and get on the back of his motorbike: a Honda Super Dream 250 cc. Do you know that the worst thing for me about the whole incident at the time was the fact that all my mates had seen me crying and shaking just like a baby? And above all, a girl I really liked had been sitting on the wall opposite and seen the whole thing. I have never been able to speak to that girl to this day.

He headed out toward what I know now to be Milverton in Somerset. We were travelling about 60 miles an hour when he started moving back on his seat. I tried to warn him that he was forcing me off the back when it dawned on me that he was actually trying to do so. I do not remember much other than my rear end hitting the back wheel and then rolling along the road. He came back and made me get back on the bike again. It was agony, and I was badly injured. He didn't care. He then took me to a children's home in Milverton and dumped me, saying and I quote: "You can have that little bastard." Apparently, he threw me across the hallway onto some tables and left (why the social worker told me that bit I will never know). I think I passed out due to a mixture of pain, embarrassment, and fear. I just knew that this was it for me as far as home was concerned.

As shocking as this may seem, I think he had planned this from the beginning. I was never part of his bigger picture, and to tell the truth, today I am glad because I really do believe that living with him through those influential teenage years could have been the death of me, either physically or mentally, and so I thank the Lord they kept me in care. These were not my best years admittedly, but at least I was making my own mistakes and not being submitted to years of abuse.

I only wish I could have seen this all back then. Unfortunately, I did not make these connections until much later in life. I worried about my mum constantly and asked every day if she had called, only to be let down gently or not so gently depending on who was on shift. I wanted so much to be allowed back to her that I think all the running away and getting into trouble was me trying to prove to him that I was a good Shorthall and that I was worthy of the family and his blessing. This was not to be, thank god, and I would spend the next three years in care. (This was extremely hard to write—even now it makes me cry thinking about how sad and lonely these years were, and how much I hated the person I was actually trying to be.)

And so my life in full-time care had begun. I was kept in Milverton for a short while, but I was soon moved to a larger home for boys called Brooklands in a town called Langport in Somerset, where I would remain until I left care in 1988. It was big children's home and it held about twenty kids ranging in age between thirteen and sixteen. I was one of the youngest, and it seemed massive. It had snooker and pool tables and an indoor play barn out the back which was big enough for five-a-side football, and it also boasted its very own assault course with a death slide. Brooklands was where I met my best friend for the coming years: Jamie Dunn. I had known Jamie before I moved back to Ireland, as he had been at the secondary school I attended before we left. Jamie was a good lad, and he helped me settle in as best as possible.

We were the youngest in the home, and so we were bullied quite a lot by the older boys when we were on our own. But I told Jamie about how my brother and I had made a deal to stick together in Ireland and how we had managed to stop the bullying, and so we decided to make a deal of our own which we stuck to until we left. Unfortunately, Jamie died a couple of years ago in a car accident during a police chase here in Taunton. I was devastated, and if I am honest, I still am. I will miss him always.

There were some good kids in there, although I do struggle to remember them all sometimes. I think I tried so hard to block many of those years out that I forgot things that I wish I hadn't. Even sitting here now, I am finding it really hard to remember, and if I am honest, it saddens me that these memories may be gone forever. I would like to say to any young people reading this who may be in a similar place to me when I was a young man to please be careful how hard you try to forget. I say this because you will get stronger and you will want to remember one day. I know this, because if you are reading this book, then you are looking for hope and you will find it—not because of my story, but because you obviously want to.

I know, for instance, that I tried to help several young people deal with being in care, especially in a semi-secure home like Brooklands, but I would not know how to find anyone of them. Except for a few of the carers, many of these people had an impact on my life, and I would love to speak to any of them and see what they have achieved in life, good or bad. When Jamie died, at his funeral I realized that all our Taunton friends were there but no one from all the years we spent in care—all those people, young and old, who had such a huge impact on our lives, whether good and bad, and not one of them was there. It shows how terrible the whole system was, how sad is it that kids just got away from the homes and never looked back.

The problem with Brooklands was that it was in a small village and everyone knew you were from the care home. We were watched by everyone all the time. Kids had done things before us, and the village hated having the home on their doorstep. So we were not allowed into the local shops without staff with us, we were not allowed to use the swimming pool in the next town because of past kids, and we were not allowed to go to the local kids discos either. And then they would wonder why, when kids did run away, they would target their cars or homes to rob.

Another serious problem I had with Brooklands was the fact that my eldest brother had been there before me. This was a problem for several reasons: number one, there were boys there he had bullied when they first got there at my age, and so payback was inevitable, and two, all the staff loved him. I got so sick of hearing how he wouldn't have behaved like me and how he was always such a nice helpful young man, which I knew was complete bullshit as he never went to school the whole time he was there and he was always on the run nicking cars or even buses. In fact, the art room wall had his name written on it and it said he was from "Tuntun"—I rest my case.

The extreme violence continued as well. I saw one of the older boys bite one of the younger lad's nose off for no apparent reason. The older lads would bully us systematically. One lad in particular was really cruel; he liked to squeeze your fingers until they were going to break and then make you call him uncle—makes you wonder why he was in care! I did get to have revenge one day, but that is not for this book.

I could not get any news from home for months when I first went into care, and so the worry about my mum was massive. I could think of nothing else. I would ask every day whether my mum had phoned, and I always had the same response: "No, sorry." Eventually I had to run away and find out for myself. I ran all the way to Taunton and hid in the bushes at the end of the street until I saw her. It was heartbreaking not being able to speak to her when she was so close. I sat in those bushes for several hours every day until I got caught and taken back to Brooklands.

I started to run away all the time then. Jamie and I began to run together so we could evade capture longer. The problem was, we were getting increasingly involved in crime and drugs whilst on the run, and so when we were caught we faced a string of offenses in the courts. Because of my past in Ireland (and I am sure because I was Irish), I was given a custodial sentence the first time, whereas Jamie was treated like the one led astray by me. This became the story of my life from that moment on, really.

School was nonexistent by this time. When I arrived at Brooklands, I did attend their school for about thirty minutes. The teacher gave me primary schoolwork to do, and when I complained, I was banned from "his" classroom. He was a complete arse anyway, and he tried to bully me into submission by putting all his weight on my foot—big mistake, and we never communicated again.

The custodial was a four-month detention center order, which I was to serve in Eastwood Park in Gloucester. It was not that bad, really—nothing like St. Pat's in Ireland—and there the problem lay. It was hard obviously, as it was prison—this was back when detention centers were still prisons. I got the usual beatings on arrival from the officers, but it was not serious in comparison, I was quite a streetwise kid, and I could hold my own or usually talk my way out of volatile situations. I also did meet a great officer here who convinced me to sit some basic exams, which I am pleased to say I passed with flying colors. He was the first person who explained to me that it was understandable that I had not coped in school, as my mind was elsewhere, and he also helped me to see that not everybody sees the worst in people. He made me believe that my time would still come; I just had to never stop looking for the opportunities in life, and to try and leave the past where it belonged . . . in the past.

When I was released from the detention center, I was taken back to Brooklands. But I absconded within hours and headed back to Taunton. My eldest brothers lived in bedsits by now, and I could visit them as long as I was careful not to be seen or people would tell my dad and he would try and capture me. Sometimes he did, and he would beat me up and tell me to stay away. I made my choice in Ireland apparently, and that meant I did not have a family anymore. My brothers in the end got tired of being a part of my beatings and asked me to stay away; they would meet me other places instead. I have looked back at these times recently, and I am amazed that I kept going. My dad during these years beat up every friend I had; he ran me over on Cheddon Road in Taunton, and he had made it impossible for me to interact with my family or peers. I was so lonely. I just became angry at everybody and would not let anyone get close enough to me to help.

Brooklands was a waste of time. My key worker was more interested in the racing post, and the people I wanted to talk to wouldn't because they were not my key worker. It was ridiculous. As well as all that, they would have meetings twice a year to plan my future that I was not allowed into. My motto was "You make your plans, and I will make me own," which I did. I was getting a taste for drugs as well about then, and I had learned that speed (amphetamines) would stop me sleeping. As I had major problems sleeping, this became my drug of choice. I hated sleep because sleep always came with dreams, and they were never good dreams, always nightmares. I would make noises in my sleep, and this had led to bullying in the past, making sleep into a serious issue for me that, as I have said earlier, I still struggle with to this day.

I would run away as soon as I got back some days—literally change my clothes, eat, and then go straight on the run again. Brooklands seemed quite happy with the situation, and so it just kept going until the police had enough charges to put me away again. On my second sentence, I was lucky enough to meet a really positive teacher, and with his help, I managed to leave having sat five more "proper" exams. They were O level equivalents, and I was so pleased with them. The fact that I managed to get maths, English, and science, and went back to Brooklands having never attended their school with more qualifications than any student they have ever had, made me feel great. I was not stupid after all!

I am really not sure how I see Brooklands anymore. It was obviously my savior but also my tormenter. At a time when good work could have been done, it was not, and the price was not only paid by me. Several dozen young people had a horrific time there during my stay, and I am sure that there were many before and many after. I saw kids attempt suicide with some pretty close results, and I saw kids neglected by a system that just did not regard us as worthy of listening to.

We told all the carers both in Olands and in Brooklands about abuse that had happened and we were never believed. The awful thing was, about forty kids kept up their stories into adulthood, and one carer (who we all knew was tampering with the little ones) was finally jailed about eight years ago for just four years after having had a long and successful career abusing at least thirty children that I know of. The police had come to see me before the trial to ask me about my time around him, but he was lucky enough to have not tried it with me, as I can say without a shadow of a doubt that I would have tried to hurt him badly. I would have known that nobody would have believed me, and I would not have let him hurt me, especially after not allowing my dad to do so anymore.

It was not all bad in care. As I have said, those years did mold me to an extent. There were some good carers whom I would love to see again, especially John Berry, Pete Allcock, and Trevor from the male team, and Jackie Spearing (whom I work with now and I love dearly). There was also Patsy who lived in Langport and Lynn Vigors, to name a few. I tried so hard to build relationships with adults, but I was never any good at it. I had lived with years of abuse, all of which had left me feeling a little unlovable and, to be honest, a bit mental.

I can remember one Christmas when it was just me and Jamie left—everyone else had been allowed home for the holidays. The staff that came on shift had volunteered to be there, and this meant that they had both mine and Jamie's full respect. It was a really nice day. We had stashed a load of cans of lager out the back, and the staff knew that we were going out for a beer and turned a blind eye. What they didn't know was that we were having a joint every time we went out as well. Jamie was given an alarm clock and some clothes, and I had a new watch and clothes but not even a card from home. We had Christmas dinner together, and because it was just two staff members and us, it felt like a proper Christmas, almost like a family. But I know that Jamie felt the same as me: deep down wishing we were at home.

I started to believe that all those years had been my fault. By my mum not calling me for those three years, she had reinforced everything that I had already thought. I had images of everyone being happier now I was not there, with my dad not hurting my mum anymore and everyone getting what they wanted. I never could trust anyone, even Jamie, which would really frustrate him, I know. It did not help that Bramwell Chapman, my social worker, would not give me any news from the house, as he was too afraid to visit and ask the right questions.

We had some great friends back then as well, and we were well looked after most of the time. I can remember friends skipping school to let us get showered and cleaned up while their parents were at work. We would eat them out of house and home in minutes, but no one seemed to mind. Some parents would let us stay if the weather was really bad, but most were terrified of the police finding out and we understood. I still see some of them around town and even speak to some on Facebook. We had several dealers who always had a floor for us in return for a couple of days of shoplifting or robbing sheds. They were not all bad people, and some did try and make us hand ourselves in, but they would not risk handing us in—they couldn't, I suppose. We once lived under a row of fir trees outside a pub for about three months and no one knew. We also lived in the back of a Skoda for a while.

It was not always pleasant though, either, and it is worth mentioning how at risk we really were a lot of the time. I can remember feeling like we were going to get raped on more than one occasion, and I even remember someone trying to talk us into pretending we were rent-boys so that they could rob the punters. We looked after each other, and if one of us got caught, the other had to hand himself in if he did not have a safe place to sleep.

We were nearly always dirty, and girls were not that interested, except for the other care girls who were always around and looking for inappropriate friendships. It was funny how we could spot each other; it was like we had a radar (or maybe we all just looked as sad as the other). I actually met some great girls in care and still remember them fondly—and I mean that in the nicest possible way. Another thing that I find really annoying about these times is again the memories; I know that we had some great laughs and that life was one big adventure as far as I was concerned back then, but I can't remember much at all.

I can remember being on the run from Brooklands and managing to hook up with a load of girls from Olands. We walked for days and slept wherever was dry. It was great fun, and it was as close to actual camping as we ever got. We all cared for each other in a way that the care system just couldn't provide. We all knew that our secrets were safe with each other, and we would talk and compare stories late into the night, comforting each other while we fell asleep. It was painful splitting up, but we knew it was time for the girls to hand themselves in, as it was getting cold and two of the girls were quite young. We walked them to Taunton social services and left them to the social workers, while Jamie and I stayed on the run.

We were kids in care and so aspirations were not for the likes of us. Instead, we lived for the moment. I did not so much want to die as I just didn't care if I did or didn't. Jamie could be brilliantly funny and was well-liked by everyone (except his family obviously). He introduced me to a wide circle of people I would not have known otherwise, and he also taught me a lot about people. He could tell what was going to happen in any situation before it unfolded. He was very intuitive, and he could read people like books. He was very rarely wrong, and I am pleased to say that he taught me this very useful skill.

We would sit on trains, sometimes all day, to avoid the weather or even just to go somewhere we had talked about in the night, and Jamie would point people out and tell me to watch them. He could then describe their body language and their facial expressions, and make a story up about their day: where they might be going and what they did for a living. I know all this was not accurate, but it was like watching a soap opera on the telly. I think Jamie knew I liked it because he always just did it and didn't wait to be asked.

I was definitely the weakest of us both, and I relied on Jamie to sort out a lot of our bother—not that I couldn't, but I just did not really like it and Jamie did it so well. He was not afraid of anyone, no matter how big or old they were. I always thought that anyone bigger was probably harder than me, but Jamie just saw them as a problem that had to be sorted and heaven help anyone who laughed at him.

We once traveled all the way to Scotland by train and didn't have a penny. We got on the train in Taunton and finished up in Glasgow. The funny thing was, we were a bit scared of the jocks because we had recently seen Jimmy Boyle's movie *A Sense of Freedom*, and so we did not even leave the train station. I can't remember how many trains we had to change to get there, or back for that matter. It took two whole days and a lot of dodgy shoplifting in towns we did not know and washing in public toilets (which was never nice, but it was an adventure), and we laughed nearly all the way

We met some great people who I have to say were not suspect at all. We had a story made up about how we had twenty pounds to buy food and drinks and how I had lost it at the train station and then the train was leaving so we got scared and just jumped on. Of course, I would be crying while Jamie told the story and there was no such thing as a mobile phone back then. People were genuinely helpful, and several of them bought us something to eat and drink, while most encouraged us to sit with them until they got off the train. We liked this because it made us look like part of a family and not look to suspect to other passengers. We hid in toilets whenever we saw the ticket master coming, and that is normally when we would change carriages and find somewhere else to sit.

Of course, nobody believed us when we got back about how far we had gotten, but my criminal record proves it, as we were caught on camera in several stations and we were charged with riding on the railways without payment several times.

We were not always so lucky, though, and we had some very difficult times as well. We were sometimes caught on the trains and kicked off on random stations in the middle of nowhere, in which case we would have to wait on another train. But in the worst cases, we were caught in the station without a ticket and made to leave the station. This was a nightmare, and we would either have to hope that whoever caught us (the guard) was about to go off shift, or we would have to try and hitchhike to the next station (which we hated doing because we knew how much more risky this was).

Hitchhiking was always dangerous and we knew it. There was always the chance of being seen and reported to the police, as well as the obvious danger of sexual predators. We would take it in turns trying to get a lift, and sometimes it would be quite quick and sometimes we would be waiting for hours—guaranteed when it was raining. We once walked from Yeovil Junction into Yeovil—it took nearly three hours in the pouring rain—only to be picked up at the station entrance by the local police and taken straight to Brooklands.

We were forever stealing to eat or get clean dry clothes, and all these offenses were piling up all the time. I will warn all young people reading this book: take heed, please, as I have been made to explain each and every one of these offenses to people I was asking to give me a job, and it has been painful to say the least. I will add, though, that the longer the gap between the interview and the offenses, the more respect I have been given and the better the jobs I have been offered. You may well have to do some unpleasant work for a few years to counter the effect a criminal record can have on employers, but it is a starting point we need and what that is shouldn't really matter.

So we were coming to the end of our time in care and eventually our time together in the way we had become used to. Jamie was offered the halfway house, which was a bungalow attached to the care home, and so he was not so keen on running anymore, as he was becoming increasingly worried about life after care and he wanted to leave with as much support as possible. And I was just being pretty horrible to everybody. I think I was burning bridges so that I could leave relationship-free.

I didn't feel like I had anyone I could turn to. I had to leave care and go into the world alone with no idea what I wanted to do. I thought that most people don't see ex-care kids as any better than ex-offenders, and I was actually both.

ON MY OWN

IT WAS NOT long after my sixteenth birthday that I wanted to leave Brooklands, and so that is what I did. I was no longer required to stay there, and I wanted to go at it alone. I have lived to regret this decision several times in my life, as I know other young people who left with support and achieved really well. I regretted it the same day, if I am honest, as that night I sat in my bedsit listening to two grown men fighting outside my door. I was terrified and I wanted to ring Brooklands and beg them to come and get me, but that was never going to happen and I knew it. My life was about to get much worse than I could ever have imagined.

Within weeks of being back in Taunton, I bumped into my mum in town. She told me to put my fag out and that just made me laugh. I told her she gave up that right years ago. We had a cup of tea in Biddy's Burger Bar and I asked her some questions, such as why she had not gotten in touch for three years. She told me that my dad had told her that she was not to contact me and she thought it would be for the best. I was kind of hoping she was going to say it was to keep me safe, but she never did. I must say, she looked tired and I felt that she wanted to leave.

I was hanging around with a lad called Neil who was all right to an extent. He sort of looked after me whilst at the same time keeping me firmly in my place. He had been friends with my older brother and they had fallen out, and I think he liked telling me what a bunch of losers my family was. My dad hated him with a vengeance for some reason and would chase us all over town sometimes. He did catch us a couple of times, and he would usually target me rather than Neil, although at least once he did catch Neil and he nearly killed him.

Neil and I were both living in different bedsits in town, and every morning we would break into another room opposite Neil's to steal some breakfast. I was in that room one morning helping myself to bacon and eggs when there was a knock on the door. I assumed it was Neil coming to help and opened the door only to see my dad standing there looking right at me. We both looked at the piece of wood that the tenant who belonged in the room had placed by the door, and he beat me to it. He beat me half to death, and Neil stayed hidden behind the door opposite. Some would say that it was poetic justice that my dad had been given the wrong room number and that I deserved the beating for robbing the room. Personally, my biggest regret is that if I hadn't been in that room, he would have left without the piece of wood, which he later beat my younger sister with.

Neil and I parted company when he went to prison. He got out and was convinced that I had tried to sleep with his misses, and so he beat me up. I think it was a good thing, to be honest. He went on to be a heroin addict, and by all accounts, he has let his girlfriend take gunshots for him—lovely man. I would probably have gone the same way if we had remained friends . . . except for the letting my girlfriend get hurt on my behalf, that is.

I ran into my dad a couple of months later. I was wondering why he called me over to his van, but fear took over and I just did what he said anyway. Looking back now, I know exactly what he was doing, but I was a little stupid back then. He must have heard that I was doing a lot of speed and he knew that all the people I was mixing with did as well. He was very friendly, and I was so taken by surprise that I could not see through it. That night he was loading me up with drugs to sell to all my young friends. Please do not judge me for this, as I was naive. I have had to bury several friends due to drugs in my life, and I have to live with the fact that some of those people had their first try with me. I have had to look their parents in the eyes and feel the resentment they had for me, and this I live with daily. I spend my life now preventing young people from going down this route, but I know that this does not change the past.

Drugs became a big part of my life, and unfortunately, I was a very successful dealer. I made a lot of people a lot of money over the following years but never anything for myself. I seemed to have a huge tolerance for drugs, and I never seemed to get the high that others got. I could eat loads and still seem to be able to function. I dealt for my dad for a short time, but he ended up turning on me and running me over again. I was injured really badly and homeless, so I was forced to look elsewhere for drugs and shelter. By this time, I had a serious speed addiction and I could not afford to live without either stealing or dealing.

It turned out that my mum had left my dad about now as well, and she was running some bedsits for a friend of hers, so I moved into one of these. My dad had been on holiday to Thailand and had gotten married to a Thai girl. My mum had found out and had finally been brave enough to leave, although her problems with my father would continue for many years yet. He would still beat her up when she was out, or he would even go to her new place to give her a hiding if he felt the need. It wasn't until her new landlord had a word that it stopped for a while, but as soon as she got a house, he started again.

One of my brothers and I did actually try to stop him physically once. He was arguing with my eldest brother in a pub when my mum walked in and got involved. My dad punched her like he would a bloke, and my other brother and I both looked at each other and the pact we made in Ireland came back, and we both moved at the same time. My brother and I landed a couple of blows, but it was not enough. He did fall to the ground, and we quickly followed his teachings and half stamped all over him. We had to leave town the following day, as he had been putting doors in all morning with, we were told, a shotgun. I could not even remember what we had done at first, but it all came flooding back pretty fast. Not our greatest family moment, to be honest, as it was in a pub full of people who already thought we were animals anyway.

I was still dealing and buying any nicked gear that I could make money on and living with a girl called Toni, whom I had met at probation. She was lovely, and I have to take this opportunity to apologize for the life she had with me. I was not in a position to have a relationship with anyone, really, and I was not a nice person to be around. I put myself and Toni at serious risk at times, and I treated her terribly. If ever you read this, Toni, I am truly sorry and I wish I could turn the clock back. You had your own problems back then, and you turned to me for help; instead, I dragged you into a vicious world of drugs and crime that you did not want or even agree to take part in. I know that Toni ended up going home to her parents, and I hope that she managed to work things out. I really do hope that she has a good life.

Toni was lovely, and I will never know why she even stayed for a second date. Our first night out included me getting stopped and searched in town. On the way home, I heard screams coming from behind a pub, and so being the hero, I ran around to help only to find it was my eldest brother beating his girlfriend up. Talk about total madness. She was having problems of her own, I think, and I must have seemed like the answer. She moved in with me, and I tried to keep myself out of trouble. Unfortunately, this meant that I was dealing, so we always had lots of unsavory characters around, which I know she did not like. She had been brought up with money, and so to have to go down a flight of stairs to use a shared shower was difficult, to say the least. She was impeccable and would spend hours making herself beautiful every day. I did love her, and I am really sorry that I was just too messed up myself to be in a relationship. Drugs were a major part of my life and they would eventually lead to us splitting up.

The police were very aware of my actions by now as well, and it was nothing for me to get raided every other week. They never found anything, but they always came back. When I was finally arrested for drugs, it was in a pub and they genuinely were not mine. A friend had to go into the job center and had asked me to hold his personal stuff while he went. Sod's law, the police came into the pub then and searched me. I got charged with supplying and was remanded into custody, which I think at the time probably saved my life. I was very ill when I got to prison and was referred to the mental health team.

Prison was a welcome respite for a while, but it was short-lived. Before long, I was back on the streets. I knew I could not deal again, as I would get a long sentence this time, and so I had to find new ways of surviving. I did try work but could not get anything, so my options were limited. I did not want to go back to bedsit land, but my options, like I said, were limited.

I was back on Cheddon Road, which was a holding pen for all the scumbags in town. My landlord (and my mother) ran about three houses on Cheddon Road, and all were overfilled and health and safety nightmares. They were filthy, and everyone in them was on drugs and or alcohol all the time—and I mean *all the time*. I can remember people boiling poppies in the kitchen and finding people comatose in all kinds of places. You could buy or sell anything on Cheddon Road or in the nearby pubs, and my mum would always buy any shoplifted stuff for a good price.

I kept changing my social circles, as people were constantly in and out of prison. This was good, as it gave me a constant change of scenery. I enjoyed going uptown, particularly to a pub called Rumours, which was run by a friend named Gary. It was a student pub really, but was home to the birth of rave music in Taunton. I loved rave music, especially the really crazy stuff. Rumours was brilliant. I was mixing with good people of my own age group who were doing drugs for recreational reasons, and this was completely different. It didn't feel as seedy, and I was not surrounded by scumbags. The patrons were really welcoming and friendly, and it felt like they were nonjudgmental.

I went to some of the best parties of my life during this time, including some really big raves. I went to prison for a few months in 1990, and the night I came out, I went straight back to partying like I hadn't been away. This was a big mistake, and I did way too many drugs. When we came back to Taunton in the morning, I went to my brother's flat for a bit of sleep. Lucky I did, because I went into a seizure and died right in front of him. He had to break my jaw to stop me from swallowing my tongue. I came around in the ambulance after being dead for two minutes.

I did meet some good friends and have some good times during this period. I was doing a lot of recreational drugs, mainly as they went well with the music, and I was managing to deal enough to live quite well, on the surface anyway. I was in debt up to my eyeballs, and certain people had been to my dad to try and get him to make me pay. What he did was buy the debts, and so I then owed him. Life became a living nightmare again, dodging dad and trying to earn where I could. This was made doubly hard by the fact my brother had threatened to kill anyone who sold me anything after I had the fit in his flat. He did care, bless him, and it nearly worked. The problem was, as we have all learned since, drug dealers don't care.

I was also quite a well-known dealer amongst the underworld in Taunton, and so being robbed was also an occupational hazard. Luckily, I had been to London with a friend of mine, Jon, and he had introduced me to the world of using liquid chemicals as weapons. I returned to Taunton fully equipped with loaded bottles of ammonia just in case of robbery. This was extremely dangerous and nearly got me a long prison sentence. I did not know that these chemicals could be classified as a firearm if used as a weapon or that it carried a seven—to fifteen-year prison sentence.

I was tested one night when I was still with Toni, and if I remember rightly, this was what split us up (and rightfully so). Five men came to rob me, but I was downstairs in another room when they came into the house and so I saw them arrive. I barricaded us in (myself, Toni, and a friend named Colin), and put Toni under a duvet in the corner. She was terrified and with good reason. It didn't take long for someone in the house to tell the visitors where we were. We were on the ground floor, and soon the windows came in and the door was being kicked off its hinges. I had to keep them out, so I kept pushing the chest of drawers against the door and told Colin to defend the windows.

Luckily, one of them was hit directly in the face with some ammonia, and it was his screaming that alerted the police to the situation. The police appeared mob handed, and the men scattered, like they do. The police had a field day taking me to the station in the hope that someone would appear at accident and emergency with ammonia injuries so that they could lock me up for fifteen years. But luckily, no one did. Unfortunately for Colin, for the police to get the door open, they had to force the chest of drawers over, which landed on top of Colin, who in turn managed to squirt himself in the face with the ammonia. I was taken to the hospital to help calm him down, as he thought that it was the robbers who had captured him.

Toni had seen enough by now to leave. I was putting her at risk, and although I was pissed off at the time, I am glad she left me then, as I still had a lot of growing up to do.

I had to get my dad's help to sort out the robbery. I knew he could make sure the damages were paid to my landlord and also that people might think twice about trying again if they thought he was involved. It meant that I was back in his pocket, but it got me away from Cheddon Road and into a shared house of my dad's. This was short-lived, as my dad started accusing me of stealing from him again and upsetting his other tenants, but the good thing was, it was the beginning of another chapter in my life.

The shared house meant that I did manage to meet a good friend again, nicknamed Puppy, before he tragically killed himself, and I also met the person I would share the next couple of years with named Stuart. Furthermore, I was starting to look at the things around me a little bit more. I wanted good things in life, and I knew that I would have to get myself sorted to get them. I started wishing that I had something to live for, someone to care about and someone to care about me. I hadn't thought about these things in years, and I thought that an offer to live in a house with a family was a sign from God that it was my time. How wrong could I be?

MAD HOUSE

MY NEW HOME was a mental institution; it consisted of my friend Stuart, his wife, and their three children. It was, if I am honest, good for me in loads of ways that were not necessarily obvious at the time. It was mental living there: the kids were fourteen, six, and four, and what they witnessed was unforgivable, although I see them now and they are surprisingly well-rounded individuals. The kids kept me together, as I soon realized that they were living a mental life and so I took it upon myself to look after them as best I could. I cooked for them daily and would take them places when I could, but I could not stop everything. Their mum was on the game, and both mum and dad were big speed users like me. There was a lot of domestic violence going on, and the eldest daughter was treated particularly poorly.

I have recently made contact with all the children on Facebook, and they are all doing really well—which, believe me, is incredible. I even named my second daughter after the two youngest. I am so proud of them all, honestly. I have always worried about them and how they would cope, but it turns out that I am not the only strong one out there. Those kids saw things that no child should ever see, and they were aware of everything that was going on. I tried my best to shelter them from the worst of it, but I was not there all the time. As it turned out, the parents split up and my friend, the dad, took custody of all three children and moved them all down to Cornwall, where I am pleased to say he managed to bring up three well-rounded young girls. I wish them all huge success in life, and I think they will manage to break that particular cycle quite well.

My mum had been given a house by the council in town, and I was slowly trying to build a relationship with her. I was visiting her daily and things were going well. She knew I was taking a lot of drugs and she did not like them in her house, which I tried to respect—although she did catch me doing amphetamine once in her front room and she split my head clean open.

A friend of mine once went into a seizure after overdosing in her front room, and I was so scared he would die there that I put him in a wheelbarrow and dumped him around the corner so she wouldn't find out. I know how awful that reads and I am truly ashamed of myself; however, let that be a lesson to you about the situations we place ourselves in. I allowed myself to mix with people who chose to chance their lives daily, and so the chances of one of them dying in my company were actually quite high. Just because you are not doing it yourself, if you are around people who are doing drugs that can kill, be prepared to deal with this kind of situation, as it is a real possibility that I have had to deal with several times.

I was going down to see my mum one day when I heard screaming coming from the street. It was awful. I knew straightaway what it was, and I was terrified. Before I even turned the corner, I was thinking about what I was going to do. As I turned the corner, I saw my dad's van parked up outside. The front door was wide open and screams were coming from within.

I ran down the close, and as I past the van I noticed that his girlfriend was sitting in the passenger seat. How surreal is that? He took his new girlfriend along while he beat up his ex-wife, and she just sat there.

I ran into the house with my heart in my mouth wondering what it was I could do. As I entered, what I saw will stay with me till the day I die. My mum was lying in a pool of her own blood and my dad was stood over her with a broken kitchen chair in his hands. I stood in front of him and my mind was spinning; I could not speak. He looked me right in the eye and said, "You're my witness, son; she hit me first." He threw the broken chair on my mum and just walked out.

My mum was unconscious, and so I phoned an ambulance. When they arrived at the house, the police were with them and they were asking me what happened. Everything that had been told to me about grassing was flying through my head until I looked and saw my mum being removed on the stretcher. Something was different; I had to help her to do the right thing. So I made a full statement and then went to the hospital to ensure my mum did the same. She had to have a lot of stitches in her head and back.

It was around this time that I met up with my wife Lisa for the first time since I had left care. I had always wanted to be with Lisa, and this was to be my chance. We had known each other for years and I always thought she was gorgeous, although I could not say so as she was three years younger than me. We had both grown up in and out of care, and she had a very brave image: shaved head and bleached blonde flat top. I loved her and I knew we would be together one day.

My way of impressing her this time was to invite her along for a day with my sister and me whilst we worked a stolen checkbook (no wonder she was uninterested). I did not even get the chance to tell her how I felt. I was arrested for the checkbook and put straight into Dorchester prison, where my dad was on remand for what he had done to my mum. This was my worst nightmare. I was terrified and I could not believe that the courts would not take this into account when sending me to prison.

Luckily, he had no idea yet about the statement I had made so I was relatively safe, although I was very aware of the fact that he could find out about it at any time. It was weird being in jail with him, but to be fair, he looked after me and made sure I did not want for anything. Luckily, he got bail due to health problems, and I was consequently moved to a young offenders' joint.

Going back to the house I was currently living in at this time with the three daughters: I feel I need to elaborate a little on this. The father was a friend of my dad's who I think felt a bit sorry for me. He had seen my dad hurt me several times, and I think it had upset him to the point that he put himself at risk by allowing me to live in his house. It was a mad house because we were all on drugs and there were three kids in the house. We were terrible role models and I knew it, but at least I tried to give them some normality when I could.

I remember stealing a roast dinner once to feed everybody and the kids telling me that it was the first roast dinner they had ever had. This spurred me on, and I made it a point to try and cook at least a couple times a week. Thinking about it now, I should have realized that the cooker had never been used before and that the kids had take away every night. This came to a stop when one day I told on one of the little ones for throwing her pizza in the hedge only to find on closer inspection that the hedge was full of pizza and kebabs. The poor girl had been hiding her food rather than admitting she did not like it.

The mother was the maddest of us all. She worked in a massage parlor by day and made everybody she could aware of the fact. She would come home and discuss her customers in front of her teenage daughter and her husband, who was not amused. You must understand that he did not like the situation and was quite happy to go to work and earn a wage, but his wife would ruin any attempt at employment he made so that she could be the martyr and go to work in the parlor. This was madness, and we all knew it because every day there would be a fight about her antics.

This went on for a considerable amount of time, and I tried to stay as impartial as I could. However, there were occasions when I had to intervene. I remember once over the summer holidays when the eldest was not allowed out at all to see her friends. Instead, she was given a list of jobs to do every day as long as Cinderella's. She did not complain, but I was very aware of the life she was living and it was annoying me that she was playing mum to her siblings. I knew it was not my place to comment, but I returned home one day to find the mother beating her up for missing one of her jobs and I lost it completely. She had thrown her daughter down the stairs, and the child was badly hurt as I entered the door. I instantly knew what had happened and I chased the mother upstairs to the bedroom. She had never seen me angry and I could tell she was frightened.

I did not want to hurt her—that was not what I was trying to do. I just needed her to know that I did not agree with what she was doing. I had to make sure she was listening. I did grab hold of her and with a little force got her attention. I told her what I felt about the way she treated her daughter, and her other kids for that matter. I knew it might mean I was homeless, but it had to be said. I told her that if I ever saw her hurt one of her girls again, I would have them taken off of her. This seemed to work for the time I lived there, anyway. She never hurt them again whilst I was around, although I can only speak for the physical abuse. I am sure the mental abuse those kids suffered was long-lasting and did not stop just because I said something.

Those kids will remain in my memory forever and I owe a lot to the family. In a strange way, their own parenting issues gave me a purpose in life, although to be honest, I was no role model myself. I think they knew that I was there for them, and I tried to bring as much happiness to their lives as I could. I would read them stories and take them to the park. I would even do the eldest's chores sometimes so that she could get some time with her friends. As I said, my second daughter is named after the two youngest and I am still in contact with the eldest girl, who against all the odds has managed to stay out of abusive relationships and turn into a good mother herself.

I must add at this point that I was no saint during this time. I was not dealing as such, but I was a very active criminal. I was surviving on opportunistic theft in town, and I would walk around all night trying to steal something to sell the following day. I was not a greedy man, and I was never out to earn thousands. I would be adding up as I went how much I thought I would get for what I was stealing, and as soon as I thought I had covered my needs for the following day, I would go home.

However, I did also have a little team of younger lads out thieving every night, and I would sell it all for them (with a big cut for myself obviously). Looking back on it, they were too young really, but at the time it didn't cross my mind. I would always try and pay them in drugs, as this would give me a second chance to earn off them, and I could sometimes earn more from them in a day than I could myself as a dealer. I suppose it was part of that particular food chain. That's how you climb out of the constant robbing yourself: by either being a fence for stolen gear or being the dealer who bought it all with drugs that you had already made your money on so that all the stolen stuff becomes your cash profit. It was a bit like money laundering really, because everyone who buys nicked gear pays cash.

I would always find buyers for whatever I had stolen and then pick it all up, preferably with them. It kept me busy and out of prison for a while. I know now that there is no such thing as a victimless crime, but I did genuinely believe back then that the police would rather I was doing what I was doing. I understand how crazy that sounds, but I actually rationalized that the reason I was not getting caught was the fact that I was doing the right thing because I was not actually dealing drugs anymore or being as horrible as I knew I could be.

However, I did eventually run out of luck, and prison was inevitable. I was involved in a serious incident with a security guard in town, and I was remanded into custody. I was in prison for a while, and this time I spent it all in Portland YOI. It was a hard prison for young people and still very Borstal-like: all single file and single cells, and no talking or running everywhere. It was known as a hard prison, and you had to be willing to fight at some point. Everyone in there was trying to prove how hard he was on the outside, and so there was a lot of testosterone about.

My first incident came about purely because I was trying to advise a young lad from Wales about prison politics and how he would have to sort a particular problem out with violence, when he decided to try and get himself noticed by starting on me in a classroom. He ran at me across the room almost bent double, so it was not really a fight, as I simply waited until he was about three feet away and kicked him straight in the face, game over. The problem was that it was in front of a female teacher, and this was considered a major incident in Portland. I was given four weeks GOAD (good order and discipline) down the block, or solitary confinement as it is also known.

I liked prison, if I am honest, because they kept you busy. You were always tired at the end of the day, and I managed to get some psychological help for the first time. I also managed to speak to my now wife Lisa by phone whilst in Portland, as she happened to be with my sister at my mother's when I had called. I asked if she would speak to me and she agreed. I told her that she was going to marry me one day.

I also sat my two A levels on this sentence. I sat English and maths papers through the education department and even managed to get myself an interview for a prison scholarship at one of the colleges in Oxford, but fear got the best of me and I never took the interview. I ended up going back to Taunton instead, and I would not even look at my qualifications for many years to come.

I wish I knew at the time that this would be my last prison sentence, as I would have saved the memories of the final few days. But alas I left and I couldn't wait to put it out of my mind.

On to New Beginnings

I LEFT PORTLAND prison in the spring of 1992, and I was different. Maybe I had grown up—I am not sure—but I had definitely changed. I did not want to go back to prison, but I still had no idea what I was going to do. Luck was, however, on my side. I managed to convince my mum to let me live with her, and this worked out quite well. Unfortunately, though, I did start using drugs again, although it was different this time around. I could no longer find old-fashioned speed; everyone was selling this new wonder drug called base. To be honest, I didn't like it from the off. It was not even made up of the same chemicals that speed was, and I knew that it was being made in town. It was really strong, and a gram would last you a week compared to the three to four grams a day I could do of speed. But it was not as clean and could make you quite ill. Lots of people were dying on it, and so I mainly did it to stop me sleeping and partly because I did not know what else to do.

I did have one major positive in my life at this time and this was Lisa. She had been living in one of my mum's places and so I saw a lot of her when I first got out and we were soon an item. I was not a good boyfriend and I was even quite cruel, if I am honest. I would meet her from work on payday and try and borrow as much as I could, and I was always arranging to meet her and then letting her down. It is amazing we are still together—as you will hear later—as I had several issues of my own yet to work through. But at that moment, what I needed was luck.

The luck came in the form of a lad from Exeter called Martin. He was a good lad, and I am sure he is still, but I have not seen him in years. He came to Taunton with a group of lads from Exeter and started seeing my sister, and this is how we met. One of his friends was out robbing cars one night and found a bag with thousands of pounds in it—£20,000 plus, if I remember rightly. I was able to convince my friend to tell me where they had hidden it, and so I did not have to do much for a while.

I was still doing a bit of shoplifting if I needed to, but I was trying my best to stay out of prison. I was happy being in a relationship, and I was trying to get it right. We were living in my mum's house in the back room, which was eventful in itself. My mum was earning good money running the houses on Cheddon Road for her friend, and she was quite the fence. Every shoplifter in town knew her, and she would buy anything. I would pick through it and try and make money selling it on, but she would eventually come home drunk and accuse me of robbing her or worse.

One evening she came home and walked straight into the front room, picked up a cup of hot tea, and just threw it all over me. I was in shock, I think, right up until she lifted the second cup and was about to throw that when I reminded her it was her settee I was sitting on. At this point, she put the cup back down, found a can of lighter gas, and split my head wide open with it. Lisa screamed as the blood flowed down my head and my mum flew into an uncontrollable rage, telling me to get out of her house and never come back.

Incidents like this may sound awful, but you got used to it, and she would always deny all knowledge that it even happened the following day. I think probably the worst thing she ever did and the one I remember the most was the night she came home drunk and woke me and Lisa up for a chat. Lisa was a couple of months pregnant, and we had stayed down there one night for some reason. My mum came back home drunk and came upstairs to wake us up. She was crying heavily, and we spent twenty minutes calming her down. She started putting her hand on Lisa's tummy and speaking to the unborn baby, but she was saying horrible things about dying and not being around when the baby was born. She went on to tell me and Lisa that she had been diagnosed with cancer and that she couldn't be cured. I was in shock at first, but then emotion got the better of me and I had to get out of there.

I walked for miles and eventually ended up back where I had stated in the park near my mum's. Lisa had been looking for me and was pleased to find me safe and not in custody. I was determined to help my mum and that she would become the focus of my life from now on. We walked back and cleaned the house whilst we waited on my mum to wake up.

When she did, it was unbelievable. She came downstairs looking pretty rough, to be honest, and we got her a drink and something to eat. She was obviously hungover and wanted to know why we were being so nice, making a point of telling us we were not getting any money because she was broke. When I told her what was wrong, I started crying, as I was upset even saying it. We told her we knew about the cancer and that we wanted to help. She went mad, accusing us both of being sick for even saying it. She said that she would never have said such a thing and that it was the worst thing I had ever done. She actually physically attacked me for this.

Lisa had had her first sight of real madness, and it would not be the last when it came to my mother. She has never admitted saying what she did to this day. I even got trouble from my brothers for saying it; no one would believe me that she had said it, even though Lisa was there with my mum's hand on her tummy.

Anyway, during this time, I was still terrified of sleep, and so I would stay up all night watching crap television or walking around looking for opportunities to earn. Martin was a good earner, and we became good friends. I knew he would get me out of any bad situation, as he was as hard as nails.

Life was about to get messy again, though. I had another fit whilst on the new wonder drug and nearly died again. My doctor was quite blunt with me and said that if I did not stop what I was doing I was going to die, and somehow I knew he was right. I was completely spun out, and again I thought it was all timing. Someone was trying to tell me something—with the fit and the baby—and it was time to sort myself out. I told everyone what I was doing and asked everyone to stay away from me.

Lisa had told me she was pregnant in December and we were determined to get it right. It was all looking good up until Christmas Day 1992. My mum had invited everyone to her house for dinner. It was the first time we had all been out of prison at Christmas for years, and she wanted to have a family day. Lisa and I were already there, and my slightly older brother arrived with his girlfriend, who was also pregnant. My sister was helping with the cooking and everyone was trying to be civil when my eldest brother arrived in a taxi with all the local alcoholics from town. He had invited them all to my mum's for dinner without even a thought. My mum was in tears in the kitchen, and I just wanted to tell them all to get back in the taxi, but my mum begged me to leave it, that she would make do.

My other brother and I just looked at each other but agreed to do nothing. We watched as he helped himself to all mum's food and drink, and gave it all out to all his so-called friends. He knew we were not happy, and he kept growling at me. He always thought that this scared me, but it was actually quite funny to see (he is also the kind of bloke who likes to rip his shirt off during or after a fight). It became too much when he went up into my mum's room and helped himself to a massive bottle of champagne that my mum had been saving, and he just opened it and started pouring mugs out for his mates.

I was fuming and my mum was in tears again. It was then that my eldest brother came in from the kitchen and walked straight toward me. He asked if he could whisper something in my ear, and like a fool, I let him. He sunk his teeth straight into my ear and started head-butting me continuously whilst still chewing on my ear. I nearly fell on Lisa, but she was pregnant so I had no choice but to try and push him the other way. I forgot I had a glass in my hand and it smashed into his neck, cutting him quite deeply. Unfortunately, he did not even notice and we fell to the floor with the television crashing with us. We rolled around the front room, and he beat me to a pulp as well as destroyed my mum's house. He eventually stopped and left my mum's house, and I went up to my room battered.

It was about a half an hour later that my other brother appeared at my bedroom door. He said that mum wanted me out and that I would have to go now. I struggled off the bed and made it to the top of the stairs before he hit me across the back of the head with an iron bar he had been hiding behind his back. Apparently, my mum had said it was my fault and that she wanted me out. I could hardly walk, let alone run, but I had to as my brother was still beating me with his bar. I was climbing over a neighbor's fence to get away when he finally stopped. I fell in a heap on the other side, and I was hurt badly. I had broken ribs, my ear was hanging off, and my pregnant girlfriend was traumatized. She helped me up when she found me, and we made our way to her mum's place, which was quite close, only to find that my eldest brother had gone there to clean himself up. I had to hide in the garden for an hour until he left.

We stayed at Lisa's mum's that night, and we moved into Cheddon Road again the following day. I promised Lisa that I would get us out of there, and I spent the next two days in the phone box finding us somewhere decent to live. I was successful in the end, and we got a shared house over in Roughmoor, which was a nice part of town. There was even room for Martin, who moved in with us for a while. The problem was that now Lisa was pregnant, and I was determined to go straight. Martin hung around for a bit, but eventually he went back to Exeter without saying a word. We woke up one day to find him gone.

We did have another tenant, a weird lad called Simon. As it turned out, he was a convicted sex offender who was being looked after by social services. He knew the day we found out, I could tell, and the following day he moved (into another area full of kids, I bet). I let a friend of mine move in for a while and that was a good laugh. He was always thieving but only low-level stuff—enough to keep him in base. He was harmless enough and his heart was in the right place. We still speak now, and he has settled down with his wife and three beautiful daughters. I am quite proud of him because I know that, like me, a lot of people had written him off. The funny thing is, just like me he just needed something to live for.

I can remember waking up one morning to the police banging at the back door. I ran downstairs to see what the problem was, and the policeman was very friendly saying that he did not want any arrests, he just wanted the coal back. I looked at him quite puzzled and said I didn't have any coal, when he told me to look over my shoulder and, sure enough, in the kitchen there was a pile of about ten bags of coal. The officer then turned around and showed me the tracks that my friend had left in the snow, which they had followed from the coal yard around the corner that led straight to our back door, and told me that I had an hour to return all the coal to the yard.

It was funny, really, and the police could have been a bit worse about the whole thing, but they saw the funny side, luckily enough.

We had another visit, though, that was not so friendly. I was awoken early one morning to find three men banging the door quite forcefully. I went downstairs ready for a fight, but as soon as I opened the door I knew not to even consider fighting. There was something about the way they asked if I was Paul Smith (our landlord) that told me just to be honest. I said I was not, and they were not convinced. I explained that it was shared house and that Paul was the landlord but he did not live there. At this point, the two bigger blokes pushed past me and systematically kicked every door in and checked all the rooms. I was made to get some letters to prove that I lived there myself. It turned out that Paul owed a lot of money to a casino on the coast and they wanted paying. It was a hardcore group of people, it turned out, and soon our landlord had no properties and no car.

I was staying away from drugs—except pot, that is—and I was not active at all. We were forced to live on our dole money, which I can assure you is not good living. Life was safe though, and it felt good not having the police knocking on the door all the time. It wasn't to last long, though. My cousin came to live in Taunton from Ireland, and we said he could stay with us. He was a nightmare. He soon got right in with my dad and was spending a lot of time up there. We had told him that he had to lie about where he was staying, and we explained the situation with me and dad. I knew in my heart that this would backfire, and sure enough, it did.

I was signing on one day in town with Lisa when I saw my dad's van parked across the street. What I did not see was him hiding by the door with a big piece of wood; he even had my name written on it. You must remember that he had a lot to speak to me about, including the beating me and my brother had given him and the statement I had made against him after what he had done to my mum. He did not hit me. He just told me exactly where I was living and told me not to make him come get me.

I knew what this meant: it meant that if I didn't go to him he would come for me and that would be worse. I knew that my cousin had grassed me up and I was fuming, but something else had changed. I was going to be a dad and I was not running anymore! I went and had a drink to try and calm down, but it was no good. I had to end this that day. I marched home and found my cousin cooking breakfast in the kitchen. I started hitting him and then told him to get dressed, that we were going to my dad's.

Lisa was hysterical by now, wondering what I was going to do, and so I sat her down and explained my plan. I would go to my dad's with my cousin, and every single blow I took I was going to share with my cousin. Lisa was to wait around the corner, and if I was not out in twenty minutes, she was to get an ambulance and get me out: NO POLICE.

I beat my cousin all the way there, I was so angry with him. We stopped at the pub for some "Dutch courage," and I left Lisa at the end of my dad's street. She has since told me that she was so proud of me, but at the time I was so terrified. I was working out what I would say, and the one thing I wanted was for him not to do it in front of all his cronies. I knocked on his back door and I could hear commotion on the other side; the door opened and there was a room full of people in there. I asked Dad straight to clear them out, which he did.

I threw my cousin in the door and told my dad why he was there. My dad laughed and said it wasn't my cousin who had told him, but I did not believe him. When everyone had left, it was just my dad, my cousin, and me. I was shaking like a leaf. My dad got up and walked toward me but then did nothing. He just looked at me, and then he said the first decent thing he had ever said to me. He looked me straight in my eye and started to cry. He said that of all his boys, he would never have given me the credit for having the minerals to knock on his door like that. I had shocked him into submission, and now that he had me, he did not know what to do with me. It was almost funny. I sent my dad's stepson to get Lisa, and the next thing you know we were part of the family.

I have never understood it. He wouldn't leave us alone. He wanted to be part of everything. He had his misses, Debbie, helping Lisa plan and get ready for the baby, and I was suddenly his best mate. It was a really confusing time, because I was still young enough to want to be accepted by him and Lisa was glad to have the company with Debbie. I stayed clean, though, and we stayed in Roughmoor right up until the baby was born.

There was to be one more low before the baby arrived and it came via the courts. I had been summoned to court for nonpayment of a fine I had been given a couple of years ago. It was only £70, so I thought I would just pay it and save myself the trouble. That would normally have been sufficient, but when I got to the courts they took the money and acknowledged that the fine was paid but said that I would still have to appear in court for the formalities. The court date was set for two days later, on a Thursday, and I honestly thought it would be all over in a second or two. How wrong can you be? I happened to get the one magistrate who wanted to know why I hadn't paid the fine weekly as ordered by the court. I was a bit taken aback, to be honest, and I was not sure what she meant, so I simply said the fine had been paid and I would like to get on, as I still had to sign on that day.

She was fuming and demanded that I be held in contempt of court. I was still in shock. Lisa was at the back of the court eight months pregnant and the fine was paid. I couldn't get what her problem was. It was then that the police arrived and took their places behind me. She had given me five days for the queen for not paying my fine weekly. I couldn't believe it, and I was very verbal on my way out of the court, I can assure you. But it didn't change the fact that I had to do another weekend in Dorchester prison before our eldest daughter was born.

We did also have a spell in a guesthouse, as our landlord had been illegally bypassing our electric meter and so we had been cut off. We were in the guesthouse on my twenty-first birthday, which was four days before my first child was due. I was convinced that she would be born on my birthday and so I did not even have a drink just in case, but it was not to be and she would be born four days later as predicted. The arrival of my daughter was the most amazing thing I had ever known. It was scary, and I would be lying if I said I was not terrified I would mess it all up somehow, but it was the most magic feeling I have ever had. I was finding it hard not to smile all the time.

However, even the most beautiful feeling in the world can be tainted very quickly, and it soon was. My eldest brother had had a son, Rory, with a girl named Jenny England whilst I was away in prison who was about twelve months old when Lisa and I got together. It was essentially a one-night stand that led to a baby. Lisa and I had helped Jenny out a few times babysitting and the like, but we never really had much to do with her. My brother was a prick as usual and had nothing to do with the baby, and she was always threatening to leave it somewhere. Anyway, my daughter was born at about 5:00 a.m. in the morning, and afterward, I headed home to get some sleep and allow Lisa to rest.

I was awoken about 8:30 am by my brother, who was frantically banging on my back door. I had no phone back then, and so by the time I got downstairs I had convinced myself that something was wrong with Lisa or the baby. When I opened the door and my brother said that Rory was dead, I actually said, "Thank god." I know how awful this sounds, but I was just relieved it was not my Lisa or the baby. Jenny had told my brother that he had died in his cot and that she was distraught. It was horrible, because everyone was mourning Rory, and I was not able to discuss my own child as it might upset my brother.

It was sickening—none of them wanted anything to do with that boy when he was alive, but they were all jumping all over the place because he was dead.

And then the bombshell came out. Jenny was arrested for the murder of Rory. The police said that his injuries could have only been caused by a blow to the head. Jenny was taken into custody, and we were all picked up and spoken to about allowing the police to do their jobs so that justice could be done. We all agreed, and the thanks we got was that Jenny was allowed to plan and attend his funeral. We do not even know where he is buried, and on top of that, she got off at court because of mental health issues.

I was so angry that someone had managed to steal what should have been the highlight of my life: my first child. Poor Lisa was left in hospital with no visitors, as everyone was too busy drinking away their feelings of guilt over Rory. Lisa never moaned, as she had no choice, but I know that she had seen the fuss made over my middle brother's baby. I know it must seem like I made a lot of comparisons, but it was hard not to. Even when we got out of hospital, we had to phone ahead of ourselves to make sure my eldest brother was not there if we wanted to visit anyone.

We think about Rory every year, as it will always be his death anniversary on our eldest daughter's birthday, but we do not dwell on it too much, as we cannot even visit his grave. I often wonder whether God just took him back where he would be safe, because he surely was not safe here. My brother learned nothing from all of this and has had at least two more kids he has nothing to do with. It is quite sad, really.

Anyway, Lisa came home with the baby and we started our battle to get a house, which turned out all right. We were soon in a two-bedroom house in Staplegrove where we would stay for twelve years. It would take some time to get used to having so much space, especially considering we had been living in one room throughout the pregnancy. We had no furniture other than what we had had in our bedsit, and so the house was bare for ages. I loved having a daughter, and it was the beginning of a new way of thinking for me. I would start to think about what it meant to be a dad and how I was going to achieve that. Maybe I overthought this a bit, because I ended up going the other way and making links to drug dealers I had not spoken to in years. It is amazing how easy it is to be a drug dealer and even to build a market where it may seem there is no need for one.

I only sold cannabis, but it was enough to keep me involved with a world that I did not want for my kids. It is strange writing this, as it feels as wrong to write it as it was to do it. Unfortunately, back then I did not have the knowledge or skills I have now, and it was the fear of not being able to provide for my kids legally that drove me to do what I was doing. I know how stupid this is now, but at the time I was trying to do the best I could. You must remember that I would not have had the confidence to apply properly for a job; I asked everyone I knew about work, but I would not have even considered applying for a job properly, as I believed that my criminal record would have ruined it anyway.

I really was convinced of these things. I thought that selling pot was the least harmful thing to do. I only sold to friends and I kept it all away from my family, but I still wanted to leave it completely behind, I just did not know how. I never stopped asking about work, though, and eventually things started to happen.

And then the worst thing that could have happened did. Lisa was suffering with post-natal depression and I was still going out with my friends a lot, leaving her home alone. It was this that my middle brother took advantage of, and he started calling around the house when I was not there. I thought nothing of it to begin with, as I knew that he had a new baby himself but as time went on, I started noticing little looks and smiles between them both. I even saw him making a point of touching her hand when she passed him a cup or an ashtray, and he was always making eye contact with her. I was paranoid anyway back then and so I told myself not to be so stupid, but the seed was planted and so I began to look for things. I would wish that I hadn't in time, because I saw more than I could cope with.

I came back from the pub one day, and the doors were open so nobody heard me arrive. I walked into the kitchen and caught them both together. It looked to me like my brother had just jumped away from Lisa, and she looked pretty sheepish to say the least. I just turned around and went straight back to the pub. My head was spinning—what had I just walked in on? And what was he doing around there, anyway? I started thinking back to all the times Lisa had phoned me recently to tell me that he was there waiting on me. My head was working overtime by now, and I was fuming. I turned around and went straight back home and just sat in silence all afternoon.

Lisa followed me up the stairs when it was bedtime and I still had not said anything. I lay with my back to her, unable to turn around. It was then that she said the one thing I did not want to hear. She first asked me what was wrong, and I still did not answer her. It was then that she said, "It is your brother, isn't it?" It was the worst thing she could have said, because in my head it confirmed every horrible thought I was having. I am not proud of what happened next, but I lashed out with my hand as I sat up and it was meant to hit Lisa, which it did. It was only a back-hander (was what I told myself), but it split her eye and that hurt me even more.

I had never hit any woman up until that point and I had always promised myself that I would leave any woman who brought that out in me. It was horrible, but just the fact that she knew what was wrong with me told me that something was up. I told her what I had seen earlier, and how I had been watching her and my brother for a while, and how I had done the working out in the pub earlier that day around how often he was calling in when I was not home. Her face said it all, and even though she swore that nothing had happened, I knew this was going to be a big problem.

I didn't believe her that nothing had happened because it didn't add up with the rest of it. She said that she had been feeling really low and that he had been being nice to her and that, yes, she was enjoying it, but nothing had happened. I became obsessed with her telling me the truth, and I would not let it go for a long time. We would argue a lot when I was drunk, and it always ended with Lisa promising to tell me the truth in her own time. I would wait for weeks sometimes and then I would erupt again and demand that she was just stringing me along and saying whatever she could to stop the arguing but that she had no intention of telling me the truth.

I was so angry with my brother, I honestly think I could have killed him. If I had the money, I think I would have paid someone to do it for me.

However, through all of this craziness, my daughter was in the middle. I knew that I needed my daughter in my life to stay focused, and I didn't see why I should have to leave. I had done nothing wrong—in my eyes, anyway. I loved Lisa and I loved the fact that I had a family. My biggest choice was whether I would let him ruin it all. I would get so angry with Lisa that she had even allowed this to happen and the fact that she was prolonging the pain by just not being honest. But my real anger was aimed at my brother, as I knew that he didn't like Lisa but only did what he did to * * *k me up. I had become as close to being like my dad as I ever wish to be. I hate that I couldn't control it and I let evil win for so long, but I was young, naive, and scared, I think, of losing the biggest positive focus I had ever had.

We argued for a long time about this nonsense, and Lisa even left once without our daughter, but I went and asked her to come home. I hadn't hit her again, and although I could be very threatening, it never worked. All the fear in the world wasn't going to make Lisa admit to something that she was adamant she didn't do. I was not sure who to believe after a while, as my brother had denied all knowledge even of the obvious flirting that I had seen. He was saying to everyone that it was all in my and Lisa's heads. I hated it, because I could not even make a decision to leave, especially if it would have meant not being sure that I needed to. They were making me feel like I was mental and that I was just being stupid.

This went on for so long that, thankfully, I had enough and decided that I had the answer. Lisa had always moaned that I had made my daughter have my surname and that her surname was different, and so I decided to ask her if she loved me properly and for keeps. I asked her to marry me, and she said yes. Looking back now, I can see that this was probably not the right thing to do, but on the other hand, at least we are still together.

The problem was that I wanted to put it all behind me and to forget what had happened before I let it destroy me (which it was doing). I let my brother back into my life mainly to prove that what he had tried to do hadn't worked, but also so I could see if there was anything still between them. I would watch him continuously . . . and her. He was a real asshole, to be honest, and he continuously watched her and smiled at her when he could. It was driving me mad, and Lisa and I would argue about it constantly when he left. She would insist that he wasn't and I was just being paranoid, but I knew what I was seeing. What I didn't realize was that I was confirming for her that he really liked her, and so she started flirting around him again. She swears to this day that she was only trying to see if what I was saying was true because I was driving her mad about it.

It was horrible because it felt like they both had me over a barrel, and although I don't think Lisa was doing it intentionally now, at the time I was convinced that she was playing games with me. Lisa knew that I would not leave my daughter, and as for him, he was just being what he is good at: a nasty, selfish piece of work. In time, all of his friends' girlfriends were targets. I know now that friends of his looked at him the same way—he is sleazy and always will be. He works that way: no morals, scruples, or even loyalty. He destroyed his own family very rapidly over the same thing, and I know that he is also responsible for splitting up several other young families. He is a loser of the highest caliber, and I will never speak to him again (but not over this—we fell out later in life).

I think the worst thing about all of what I just wrote about was the start my first daughter had in life. It was killing me at the time, and the guilt I still feel is huge. I should have left rather than staying and fighting every day; that is what I would have told myself to do in an alternative universe. But unfortunately, I didn't have the wisdom I have now, and I was scared and angry that I should have to lose anything. I tried to tell myself that the wedding would fix things, and so I just focused on that.

It was on the weekend before the wedding that things nearly ended for Lisa and me. My brother was in my front room and Lisa was climbing the stairs, and of course, I was watching the pair of them like a hawk. I saw Lisa when she thought she was out of sight drop on the stairs to try and catch his eye. Again, I said nothing until later on, and then I told her what I had seen. She swore that it was not what I thought and that she was just trying to see if what I was telling her about him always watching her was true. I was so confused that I didn't really know what to do. I couldn't understand why she would do that knowing that I would be watching and also that I would go mad. It didn't make any sense, but again I was being told by Lisa that it was me that she wanted to be with. The wedding was only days away, and my daughter was all ready to be a bridesmaid, even though she was just eighteen months old. Everything was arranged, and so I went against everything sensible in my head and we went ahead with the marriage.

Lisa has never really understood why that look on the stairs that day meant so much to me, but the simple truth is that I will always wonder "what if?" What if he had been looking at her? What if he had told her he loved her? What if I was second best because he wouldn't leave his own misses and kid at the time? He hated that I was telling everyone what he did, and he was making a point of telling everyone that Lisa was a monster he wouldn't touch anyway—and I was telling this to Lisa, which I am thoroughly ashamed of now. Lisa had postpartum depression at the beginning of all this, and I was trying to be as cruel as I could be. I am not proud of myself and I have since tried to make up for this, but I know that Lisa still has many reasons to hate me.

And so you can see how difficult this was for me—who was I to believe? Was it Lisa who was after my brother? Or was my brother after Lisa? Were they hiding it because of public opinion? I would never know, and the worst thing is that I still don't to this day. We do not talk about it much, but it is always there in the background. My brother is no longer part of our lives, thank god, but the memories of the early years of my eldest daughter's life will never leave me.

I think I have just tried my best to rationalize my behavior back then, and I feel that before I move on I should be slightly more honest about my own actions. I didn't spend much time at home once my daughter started crying more, and it was easy to leave Lisa on her own all day with the baby and just convince myself that she was happy to do everything. I should have noticed that she was so depressed, but I was still way too selfish back then for that to even cross my mind. I thought that she would be so grateful to have a bloke like me—the great catch that I assumed I was for Lisa. It was funny, but I thought just agreeing to be a dad made me some kind of martyr.

I really was oblivious to the fact that Lisa needed attention, and so it was easy for my brother to manipulate the situation. And I was not brave enough to just confront him with my anger, so I took it out on Lisa. I would bully her for hours sometimes, trying to make her confess to having an affair with my brother, and I never believed her when she sobbed that she hadn't. I should not have said what I said above about never knowing, because deep down I do know that she didn't do anything. I also think that she would have told me by now—maybe not back then when I would have been too angry to deal with it. But we have been truly honest with each other in recent years, and I truly believe that she has always loved me and that I was a fool for not seeing that instead of focusing on all the negative horrible things I let myself imagine and then act on.

Anyway, back to our wedding, a story that just has to be shared. The wedding was a joke, to be fair. We got married in a Catholic church, as I thought this was what I was meant to do. We managed to do it quite well considering we had no money. Lisa had a new dress, although not exactly what she had her heart set on, and my sister managed to change the price tags in the shop on the bridesmaid dresses for the girls. I had let my parents get involved in the wedding, which was our first mistake. They had booked the cheapest venue in town, and my mum had taken it upon herself to invite every dirty alcoholic in town to the reception.

It was awful. We knew most of them from growing up, and we did not want our reception to be hijacked by them. My dad had also decided to change the music arrangement we had made with a band that we liked and replace them with a crappy disco and an Irish singer. The finish for me and Lisa was when the Irish singer started singing "Divorce," an old Irish song, whilst wandering through the tables. I had to laugh, but only for a minute.

I found Lisa and asked her to start telling people that we were leaving to start our own party somewhere else. She was shocked but agreed, and we began telling all our friends that we wanted to leave and go to our local pub away from all the drinkers who would not even know we had left. It was about now that everyone started chanting "Speech!" I made a very quick one—I won't repeat what I said, as it was not very nice. But the rest of the day actually went really well, and we went on a short honeymoon at Centre-Parcs in Longleat Safari Park in Wiltshire. It was lovely. We had a nice log cabin in the woods, and we agreed to try and put everything else behind us for our daughter's sake. I am glad we did.

Obviously, we didn't go home as different people, and it would take us time to really put things behind us. We both would have a lot of lessons to learn over the coming years, and we would need to rely on each other more than we ever imagined. I will always be sorry for the way I handled things, but all I can say is that it was all part of the character building journey that has been my life. Maybe I had to see the dark side of myself to really understand how easy it is to let yourself replicate a life you were convinced you would never be capable of living. I won't pretend it was easy, but we did get through and we are thankfully still together.

Working Life

My FIRST PROPER job was working for a friend of mine named Sid who had his own tree surgery company. He paid peanuts, but then again, he climbed like a monkey. The problem was, he was awful to work for because of the way he spoke to me on the job. He was always shouting and swearing at me, and I would go home fuming sometimes, but I did like the fact I was working. We worked together for some time, and it was all right but not really for me, if I am honest. My second daughter was on the way, though, and I needed to be in work of some kind, and I was still not confident enough to apply for a real job.

Our second daughter came five years after the first, and I think that was a good gap between them. Lisa and I had not gotten off to the best of starts, and the fact that we were too young to be parents and had few or no parenting skills that we were aware of didn't help. But we were really trying now, and we had started getting help for our own issues. I had asked for some counseling sessions about my anger, and Lisa started a very long and sometimes very emotionally draining personal recovery program. It was the best thing she ever did, and there has been no stopping her since. She is still going from strength to strength work-wise and academically, as she has just been awarded the highest mark ever awarded on her final assignment for her diploma. I am very proud of her, and I hope she goes on to do all the other things she has set her mind on.

We both knew what it meant to be real parents, though, and I really believe that we did try our best against all the odds. I know I have made some mistakes and Lisa and I have had our fair share of arguments and fights, but we have always made a point of letting our kids know that we are in control and we love each other whatever we say in arguments. It is that concern that I think has kept us together for all these years.

I know some people would argue that it is never better for the kids for parents to stay together when things aren't necessarily going well and they are arguing. However, I personally think that they are wrong. I thought marriage was a "for better or worse" deal, and although I am no Catholic by any stretch of the imagination, we have tried to work through our problems and our kids have seen us do that. Lisa and I had never been happier than we were at this point when my second daughter was born, and hopefully we taught our daughter to not just start families and then give up at the first major hurdle.

Let's face it: all marriages have their own disasters, and we have to teach our children that getting married and starting a family is a responsibility that needs to be thought through and worked at if it is to succeed. I am not saying that people should tolerate any form of abuse; in fact, I would say that we should have a 999 system in place to stop domestic abuse, where people are paid to put a stop to this. What I am saying is that if we do make the decision to start families, then we owe it to our kids to try and resolve any issues before we give up and move on.

I do feel, though, that if there is still love between the parties and they can recognize the problems and want to fix them, we need as a society to make this kind of support more accessible and even more acceptable as a form of help. There is still a major issue with how many people use mental health services; many people do not even want to be seen going into the offices, let alone admit to needing treatment or counseling of some kind. It was hard work getting to see an actual psychologist in my own case, and I think this should not be up to a GP to determine. I think that there are a lot of people with serious anger issues in prisons around the country who have asked to see a psychologist and were offered counseling instead.

I am not knocking counseling at all; I have used good counselors several times in my life and I would highly recommend it to anyone. What I am saying is that if a man is sitting in front of you (and I am speaking from experience) saying, "I am really worried about my anger. I am not able to contain myself when my temper takes over, and I lose control completely. I want to see a shrink," don't take a chance and see if he wants counseling.

I knew what I needed and it was not counseling. I had been there and done that before. I needed to sort out my thought processes and be able to see how my head worked before I could ever get a handle on my temper. In the end, it took a disability before I got see a psychologist. I must confess to hurting several people between the time I first asked for some proper help and when I finally got what was actually less than six months of cognitive analytical therapy—which completely changed my life, and my families' lives for that matter. I can't help wondering what my life might have been like if I had been given the cognitive understanding I have now earlier in life. Sorry if that was a bit of a rant—it is something that really annoys me, as I know many people who will share similar stories but with sometimes much more tragic endings.

Lisa and I have grown in love rather than starting out that way. We were both scared kids to begin with. Our parents were useless, and in fact, my mum had told Lisa not to rely on me, that I would be gone as soon as the baby was born. How wrong she was, and how glad I am that Lisa told me that she said it, because I am sure it helped me stick it out. We both knew that we wanted to be great parents and that we wanted to be with someone who felt the same way. Of course, we said we loved each other in the beginning and we went through the motions; what I am saying is that now that we understand what love is, we can say it and mean it.

We were amazed to get another girl, and to be honest, I was glad, as it meant my eldest would have company. My newest daughter was beautiful and so quiet; she was so different from my eldest, it was incredible. She was really lazy, in no rush to walk or talk, just happy to sit and watch her sister run around for her. I was really enjoying being a dad, and I think I was getting much better at interacting. I struggled playing with them in the beginning, as I didn't have any knowledge to draw upon, but I became a dab hand at dressing Barbie and playing with Polly Pocket.

I was then offered a chance at a great job. A friend of my wife had started seeing a man who was a stone mason. He seemed like a nice chap, and so when he offered me the chance to go and work with him, I jumped at it. It was a great job, and I really enjoyed working with stone. We were working in Cheltenham, where we rebuilt the main spire of a big Catholic church. I loved being a stonemason, and although I was not best friends with

Rueben, the boss, come the end, it was a shame to leave. Unfortunately, the job finished and there was not enough work locally to keep us on.

I went back to work with Sid, and he told me that if I did my street-works qualifications, he could set me up with my own van and that the money would be much better. I saved up, went on a training course, and came back with all my certificates just to be told that there was no job. I was pissed right off, to be honest, as it felt like my hard work and money had been wasted.

I had not considered the fact that the street-works qualifications had made me very employable until someone else told me so. I was finally brave enough to try and actually apply for advertised jobs. Since then, I have gotten every job I ever applied for, believe it or not, and sometimes even had a choice of jobs. I was not earning great sums of money, but I was earning enough to be able to be clear of benefits, and more importantly, I kept myself away from dealing for several years for the first time in our lives. I was really starting to think about what I might be able to achieve with some hard work and a bit of luck.

I wanted to work with troubled kids and kids in local authority care, and deep down I always had. I was not sure that I would be allowed to, and so I got in touch with my old head of care, Mervin, to ask for his help and advice. He was surprisingly pleased to see me and wanted to meet Lisa and my daughters to see for himself the success that I had made of my life. He was genuinely pleased to meet Lisa and see that we had managed to stick together against all the odds. It was funny hearing him tell Lisa stories about my time in Brooklands and to hear him laugh when he told them.

It turned out that although Jamie and I had believed we were the worst kids they had ever had, we were actually far from it. He reminded me of times and people I had not thought about in many years. He reminded me of trips to Blackpool to see the illuminations and also to Alton Towers, and best of all, he reminded me about a camping trip we all went on in the Wye Valley in Wales. It was a canoeing holiday, and I hadn't told anyone that I couldn't swim, so I created a big scene so that I could throw my canoe down in a strop and refuse to take part—of course, blaming whoever it was who had upset me for ruining my holiday.

The funny thing was, Mervin said that he knew exactly what I was doing. It is funny how when we are kids, we can convince ourselves that we are the first person to ever feel like we do and so we must be the first person to act it out in a certain way. I like to see myself as someone who would be able to read that situation just as well if I had seen another young person behaving the same way in a similar situation because I have lived it. But what I have learned is that actually there are good people out there who don't need to have lived things to understand how they might affect young people. Some people genuinely can see behind behaviors and instinctively know when something is not quite as it may appear.

This is really important for me to share, because what I am trying to say to young people who may be in a bad place whilst reading this book is, there are some good people in the care and related industries, even though they may not appear to be from a similar background or environment. I never believed for one minute that Mervin had seen it all before, and yet he was bloody good at his job. I say that because he knew that there was no point in trying to explain things to me since I wasn't listening anyway. He, like me, believes in timing, and he said that he knew that I was not ready to be helped, which is why he recommended custody—not because I was the worst kid in care, but because I needed to be kept safe until I was ready to accept help. That last bit completely knocked me off my feet, because I just knew that he was telling the truth and I finally realized what a difficult decision that was for him to make—not the easy option I had always believed it had been.

I was forever running away from his care to live with some very unsavory characters and building a huge criminal record, and Mervin knew that if this continued, I would be beyond saving. If I was not locked up and if I had not met the key people I identified earlier, then I would not have sat those exams, would have still had zero self-esteem when I left school, and would have continued to avoid anything even slightly challenging. It was those initial exams that gave me the confidence to do others and even to do all my street-works qualifications—not to mention writing this book.

I believe that tough love has its place and that sometimes when we are young we need people like Mervin who are willing to stand there and take the abuse from us when they make tough decisions about our care. I love Mervin now for everything he did for me, and I am truly sorry for the way I behaved around him. But the point is, Mervin doesn't want me to be sorry; he knew I didn't mean it back then, and he certainly hasn't judged me on my behavior. He was a professional at the top of his game, and he did the right thing for all of us boys to the best of his abilities. It is amazing to think that I am one of his success stories and that he is aware of it. It makes me smile knowing that maybe he saw the good man in me years ago and that he was purely guiding me on my way.

So back to my story. I had a friend who was working for a private-sector care company, and he said that he would get me an application form. I was really nervous putting my application in, and I did not hear anything for several weeks. However, eventually the phone did ring and, to my surprise, I was asked to do a trial shift starting that day. I was sent to a flat in Taunton, which was being used as a satellite provision for a teenage girl. I arrived to find the young person dismantling the front room, and all of the staff on shift there had locked themselves in the staff room.

I amazed myself at how well I took control of the situation. I asked the young person to remove herself to her bedroom whilst I sorted things out. She obliged, but I think more because I was a stranger than because of my air or authority. I asked the staff team to come out of the staff room, which they did, only to tell me that they were going off shift and that someone would be with me soon. I managed to convince one of them to stay with me until the relief arrived by explaining that I had not even been interviewed for the job and that this was meant to be a trial shift. It transpired that most of the carers had been employed in much the same way.

I did have a kind of interview during one of my shifts one day, but it was more of an induction than an interview. I was so pleased to be given the job that it didn't really bother me at the time, but all these things I would eventually come to see as quite obviously wrong. I loved the job, though, and all the young people were fantastic in their own ways.

This particular company was catering for some extremely damaged young people who were all meant to be double staffed at all times—both to protect the young person and also to protect the carers. To begin with,

I was always partnered with someone, as I was meant to be learning the job. But all I was watching was carers either coming on shift with a bag of DVDs or computer games that they would expect the young person to entertain themselves with or playing silly wind-up games with the young people trying to get them arrested so they would have an easy shift.

A shift was meant to start at 10:00 a.m. and run for twenty-four hours until 10:00 a.m. the following day. I was very conscientious and would not leave until a replacement arrived, but some carers would just leave at 10:00 a.m. regardless of someone taking over or not. I would show up for work expecting a handover from whoever had been on shift only to find the young person by themselves. The worst thing was, you never really knew when the staff had actually left.

It was incredible talking to the young people about their home lives and what had led them to being with us, and it was the beginnings of me seeing the amazing similarities between them all—such as social deprivation and drug and alcohol abuse. I found it incredibly difficult learning that my experiences and how I dealt with them were individual to me and that, although we may all have shared certain experiences, we all internalized them very differently.

I was genuinely amazed at what some kids could cope with and still be able to have enough sense and focus to not allow it to control them. I thought to begin with that a lot of it was just bravado, but I soon learned that actually it was resilience and a determination. I think my obsession with remembering as much as I could to prevent myself from ever making the same mistakes actually just resulted in it controlling my whole young life and me not ever actually allowing myself time to relax and enjoy life. Their ability to carry on was a gift that I wish I had had.

I met some amazing kids whilst working for this company, but some of the so-called carers were driving me slowly insane. It amazed me how they could call themselves carers and then pick and choose which kids they would work with, although I must add that there were several really good carers on the team as well—just not enough to make a big enough difference. For all the good work you and others could do, there were several people doing their best to undo it on the next shift.

They all had their favorites, and most would refuse to work with any of the young people who didn't like them or who displayed any kind of challenging behavior. I ended up working with all the young people no one else wanted, and sometimes I would have support and sometimes I would be alone with up to three young people. I would, of course, complain, but they knew I was the kind of carer who would not just get up and leave, and so they took advantage. It was not just me they treated like this; the longer I was with the firm, the more I realized that they treated all their good staff this way.

I was trying my best to ignore the fact that the system was awful and that people were making a lot of money out of these kids who were being seriously shortchanged. I saw carers arrive with all their laundry from home at the beginning of their shift and spend the entire shift doing it. I saw kids being arrested because carers would deliberately wind them up. For example, I was on shift one day when a carer blackmailed a young person into doing some work with the promise of KFC (Kentucky Fried

Chicken), and then when the food came, she tried to get the young person to make her a drink before he could have his food.

He refused, saying that he had already earned the food, and when she wouldn't let him have it, he went crazy. She then phoned the police, and when they arrived, she offered them his food. That poor lad spent the night in the cells with no tea because she was a control freak. I must add that this was right at the beginning of my job and so I didn't feel like I could intervene. If it had been after I had been there for a while, I would have had the carer arrested or, even better, sacked.

However, thanks to my time with this company, I completed some amazing training with PRS (Personal Recovery Service)—a company in Somerset that works with abused and damaged young people—for which I will be forever grateful. The lady who ran the training and indeed the entire project was truly inspirational. I really enjoyed learning about the different programs that they ran at the center, such as the crockery room where young people could express their anger whilst going through a counseling program by smashing plates and bowls. There was also a painting room and a fiber optic/sensory room, a padded room, and a room full of punching bags. All these were put in place to ensure that every young person or adult could find a way of expressing themselves safely. This is an amazing center that does some fantastic work, and I promise that if this book is a success, a percentage of any earnings will go toward ensuring that PRS is there to support young people long into the future.

We were working with some extremely damaged young people and, if I am honest, young people whose lives really did help me put my own life into perspective. I know that all abuse in whatever form feels the same to the young person involved—for instance, to never, ever have any physical contact from your father can feel just as bad as years of inappropriate contact. I suppose I mean that the resilience that I saw in these young people reminded me of why all those years ago I thought it was important to remember my own childhood—not so that I could be a martyr to it, but to ensure that I did not replicate the situation. If I was going to do it differently, I would need to raise my game quite considerably.

However, I loved the job I was doing and I really believe that I was having a profound effect on the young people I was working with. I tried to keep my past out of it, but inevitably people would start to quiz me about my name. I would tell people why I was doing the job and bits about my past, but I could tell that people were loving being able to spread rumors around the company. This would be my eventual downfall.

I was getting increasingly recognized by management as being good at my job. I was sometimes working sixteen twenty-four-hour shifts a month, and I was working with the kids no one else would work with. At the same time, I was very confident when it came to whistle-blowing on my coworkers' bad practices. I had witnessed plenty since I had been with the company, and I had said to management that if I was to be running a house, then it would have to be my way. They agreed, and so when I arrived at a house and found things like washing up rotas and laundry rotas, I would remove them and insist that we worked as we would at home. This infuriated some of the other house managers, and they soon began complaining about me.

I had one female carer who refused to drive the car but would not get in the back seat, saying that she would look like—and I quote—a twat. So what, I ask you, would that make the young person if he himself sat in the back?

That to me was bad practice, but it was not worth a fight, so I explained that I would sit in the back if she was that bothered, but she still held that she didn't want to drive. I went straight into the house and phoned the manager, who then ordered my colleague to either drive the car or get in back. He also reminded her that the car was provided for the young person and that she was paid to keep him happy and entertained.

The problem was that I was doing a lot of things like this. They all seemed totally justified to me at the time, but although all the kids thought I was great and so did the managers (because the kids did, and so their social workers were happy and they were getting paid), I was not popular amongst some of the staff. It came to a head one day when I was called into the office and asked to sit down. Someone had took it upon themselves to inform all the different social services departments that placed young people with the company about my criminal past and my history of drug use and dealing. I was gutted, to say the least. I know who did it, and I will never forgive her, but the damage was done. I was not the only person they stitched up either—they had dug up information on three of us and we were all called in for the same chat.

It was over. One by one, all the different social services departments requested that I not be allowed to work with the young people they were placing, and so slowly, there were no more kids I could work with. It didn't matter that I was keeping kids who had never stayed anywhere more than a week for months at a time; it didn't matter that I had gotten kids into school who had never been; it didn't matter that I was building relationships where none had ever existed before. All that mattered was my past, and there was nothing I could do about it. The letters were not even signed and so should have been treated as the malicious spiteful letters that they were.

It would have been nice if someone at least came to see me or even ask the young people I was working with about my history and how it was that my past helped to form the highly effective relationships that I was able to build with these young people.

I was given a light maintenance job, but I hated how I had been treated, so I left and began another journey on the roads and highways of Somerset. I wanted to try and use the street-works qualifications I had achieved before the care job had taken over, and so I started looking for ground works jobs in the papers. I had to take a couple of really bad jobs before I was lucky enough to get a job with a big South West company working on the highways.

But before I got that lucky break, I had applied for a job over in Sherbourne advertising for a ground worker. The boss asked if I had any experience, and of course I lied and said loads. When I arrived to start work the following week, he met me at the side of the town hall in Sherbourne, and I realized that he was intending to leave me to own devices. He was telling me the dimensions of a massive car park and fence that I would be putting in on the land we were standing on. I was just about to tell the truth and admit that I didn't have a clue about what he was saying, when a JCB turned the corner and joined us. The boss then explained that someone else would be arriving with a load of scalpings (stone and sand for compacting earth) and another laborer with a roller. I thought, to hell with it, I might as well have a go.

It was easy to begin with as I just had to get the JCB to level the land ready for the stone to arrive and then make sure that the stone was dropped all over the site to save moving it twice. All was going well so far, and then about a thousand curb stones arrived and I was informed that the whole car park was to be edged with the curbs before we could roll out the scalpings. It was all over, as I had never laid curbs in my life, let alone a thousand that had to be filled with scalpings and rolled. I was about to give up and confess when the JCB driver climbed out of his cab and started setting up the first curb. I walked over and was about to inquire when he put his hand up and stopped me. "You haven't got a clue, have you, son?" he said. "No," I replied, "but it can't be that hard surely." He looked at me for a minute and then nodded and began to laugh.

He asked me how I managed to get the job if I didn't know what I was talking about, and I explained that I had lied about my experience. He was brilliant about it and explained that we all have to lie to get work sometimes. He even admitted to not being qualified to drive diggers for years before anybody thought to ask him for his papers and he was forced to do his qualifications. He taught me a lot, and that is why I wanted to remember him in this book. The company, however, I was not with for too long. The pay was bad, and it was a long way to drive every day, so I was constantly looking for another job.

I actually nearly died going over to work in Sherbourne one day. I can remember seeing a lorry some way ahead of me on the main road into Sherbourne, and the next thing I knew I was waking up and the lorry was about ten feet ahead of me. I skidded for what seemed like an eternity and came to a stop right underneath the back of the lorry. I was shaken up quite badly, and I knew then that all the traveling was getting to me. I had been leaving at 6:00 a.m. every day to get on site for 7:30 a.m., and I was not getting home till 8:00 p.m. most nights. It was too much, and the money was not worth dying for.

I was getting braver in terms of what I was willing to apply for, as I was learning that I was a hard worker, and I always seemed to get the jobs, so I knew I must interview well. And so I began looking for work with big companies like Wessex Water and British Gas and the other utility companies, as I knew they paid really well and I would be picked up from home.

Eventually, I was lucky and I got a job with a big company following the gas and water crews and refilling the roads after they had finished digging them up for repairs. It was a brilliant job and I loved it—I still keep in touch with the gang I worked for—and I was on a decent wage for a change. It was not really hard work, although it kept me fit and the camaraderie and banter were brilliant. We worked all over the South West and it was never dull; sometimes we would be part of a bigger gang and so the competition aspect was always there amongst the gangs as well. The best gangs got offered the overtime on the weekends, and this was worth big money that we all needed.

All was good for a while until one day something really odd happened. I was compacting a load of stone in a hole just outside Taunton when I had some kind of seizure. My friend Simon, whom I was working with, said that my eyes just rolled into the back of my head and I threw myself backward and started banging my head on the road. I had to have about nine stitches and about six months' worth of medical tests just to be told that they didn't know why it had happened and that it was either due to the vibration of the tools we were using or a result of the years of abuse my body had suffered.

It was horrible, because we did not know what was going to happen. Lisa was scared, and I was not sure I wanted to go back to work with the threat of it happening again, especially not working on the highways. But we needed a source of income. In the end, it was a friend who came up with the solution. I had several years before tried to start a business up in Taunton that I had seen in Amsterdam. It was a service that used collapsible mopeds to get people and their vehicles home if they had been drinking alcohol. I was convinced that I could make it work anywhere, but I could not raise all the funds needed at the time. I had even managed to do an NVQ 3 in Business Management and Ownership with Business Link in Taunton (I had convinced the job center that it was my only chance of employment due to my criminal past).

I submitted a business plan to the Prince's Youth Business Trust, who I must say would have given me half of the funding I needed, but unfortunately the banks would not give me the rest. In fairness, I was really nervous in the bank, and I think I probably let myself down a little. To be totally truthful, my business plan was pretty awful, looking back on it. Knowing what I do now about banks and having learned how to write, I would never have submitted what I did to the bank if I had known. Let's just say that I still had a lot to learn about presentation skills.

However, someone else had been to Holland and had the same idea as me but had taken it to London. It turned out that they had made it work and were featured on the *Richard & Judy* show one night. I got a phone call from an old friend who had seen the program and wanted to talk to me. His name was Nigel, and as I was going to be at home anyway due to the seizure incident, he was willing to remortgage his flat and fund the business if I could run it from home. This was amazing news, and it would give me something to focus on whilst they figured out what the fit was all about. At the same time, it gave me a huge confidence boost—someone was willing to invest their own money with me!

Nigel put 20,000 into the pot and we negotiated a good price for the bikes and sorted out staff. We put all the drivers through intensive driving courses so that the insurance to drive any vehicle could be kept to a minimum. It was a great idea, and the local news and radio did big stories on our battle against drunk driving, but alas it was not meant to be.

We worked hard to promote the business, pounding the streets leafleting doors and shops. It was just not going to happen in Taunton, I think. We priced it cheaply to try and guarantee business, but as it turns out people expect to pay more for good drivers and so were frightened that we just had a load of cabbies or something similar. We kept the business running for about fifteen months, but we did not make any profits at all. We were able to claim some of our losses back against our tax from other jobs, but we still lost several thousand pounds. It was a great experience though, and I think I managed it really well. Nigel and I are still good friends, and we would do it again if we had the time (and just be a lot more expensive next time).

I was speaking with lots of specialists during this time, and eventually it was decided that it would probably be safe for me to return to my manual work. I couldn't wait, and it felt so good to be earning again that I was quite surprised at the change in me. Who would have thought that I would want to go to work, let alone put myself at risk in order to do so? It was good to go back to work, but it did put a lot of pressure on Lisa, who was left to man the phones for the business, and I ended up working all hours to maintain my job and run the business when I finished work. It was a sad day when we did finally decide to shut the business lines down, but even our accountant was suggesting that without a massive cash injection we would be better off accepting defeat and calling it a day.

What my immediate family thought of me was really important, and I was beginning to realize that I liked my kids seeing me going and coming home from work and how I had never seen that growing up. Where I grew up, nobody worked and everyone seemed to be in the pub all day, and so to me, work was for mugs. I literally thought you left school, got your social security money, and went to the pub. Aspirations were not for the likes of us, and anyone who did work did it for cash.

I was starting to realize that my kids were learning all the time and watching everything I did. This was quite strange because it meant that although I thought I was a very conscientious dad, I was actually a parent who thought that kids do not notice things. I think I was just beginning to realize what a massive impact I had been having. I had up until this time still been smoking lots of cannabis and also drinking a lot—I had to have at least four cans of lager a night or I was convinced I would not sleep. And all the time, my daughters were seeing me do these things. They were now ten and five years old, and believe me, I was beginning to really worry about what my eldest would think a good man was and whether what she had seen as a child would influence that. Today, I can only hope that she will be more influenced by what I have achieved since.

Another year passed. Lisa was pregnant with our son at this point, and we were really excited. We had found out what it was for the first time, and I must add that we wished we hadn't, as it took the excitement out of the pregnancy. We spent the rest of the pregnancy just waiting for him to arrive without the excitement of wondering what it was. However, he was so worth the wait, and I felt like I had earned my son. I had done ten years of Barbie and Polly Pocket, and I wanted to buy some boy toys. I couldn't wait until Christmas.

In terms of work, I was still experiencing the never-ending stream of luck that is my life. I had been back at work for some time when we got a new manager called Paul. I didn't like him from the start. He was trying too hard to be everyone's mate. It was all right to begin with, and then we started noticing the cutbacks he was making. For instance, there were no more new replacements when machinery was broken; instead, we saw a load of reconditioned whackers delivered and we were given one each.

The first problem was they were "elephant feet whackers" that, for those of you who do not know, are different from normal whackers in that they have a much wider foot. They were made for trench lines and not for the kind work we were doing, which were patches that were normally square or rectangular in shape. The elephant foot whackers were too hard to control in the patches we worked in, and they were much harder to get on and off the lorry every time we had to stop. We had complained several times to our new boss, but we were told to make do. It was an accident waiting to happen . . . to me.

It all came to a head when we were working up in a place called Poulton in Wiltshire on a little B road, and we were under strict instructions that the road had to be opened that day as it was a Friday and it was a main commuter route. The water company had been digging all week, and we had about ten tons of tarmac to get down in about six hours. We cracked on as we did normally, but it was raining and some of the holes we were in were over six-feet deep and they were not shored up either (supported by timber framing to prevent landslides). We were struggling trying to get the elephant foot in and out of the holes, and we were knackered by lunchtime.

I was working alone with the whacker following the lorry with the aggregate that we were using to fill the holes with. I was about a meter down in a hole in the middle of the road that was made up of big boulders, trying to keep control of the elephant foot and stop the thing from getting stuck under one of the rocks. Suddenly, it caught it itself under the edge of one of the bigger stones, and within a split second, it came down on the top of my right foot. It tore right through my steel toe caps, crushing my right foot. It took all my strength, but I managed to throw the whacker out of the hole and it landed in the middle of the road. I was screaming now with pain, and I could see my foot was in a mess even through what was left of my boot.

I managed to drag myself out of the hole, and by then some of the gang had made their way to me and were trying to carry me back to the lorry. It was agony climbing into the cab, but I managed it with help and managed to get my boot off. My foot swelled up immediately, which seemed to ease the pain a little. A first aider came down from the water gangs and asked whether I thought I needed to go to hospital, but me being the hard man that I was decided I would be fine and that the road needed to be opened.

I sat in that lorry cab for six hours whilst my gang finished the job, and then we set off home to Taunton. It was on the way home when I was speaking to Lisa about the state my foot was in and the fact that I would be unable to work for a while that the question of pay came up. Lisa was concerned, as our son was only two weeks old and it was only five weeks until Christmas. I telephoned my boss just to check, but as I had been hurt at work, I was sure it would not be a problem.

I was in for a terrible shock. My boss informed that since everyone liked to claim for any injuries nowadays, the company as a rule did not pay people who were off through work injury anymore. Apparently, they paid statuary sick pay and advised people to make a claim. I was very distraught and even offered to sign a disclaimer if they would just pay my wages whilst I was off, but there was nothing he could do—it was policy and that was that. I even pointed out the fact that I had sat in the lorry all day and got the road opened, thinking that might make a difference, but to no avail.

I was only glad at this point that I hadn't made it home, as I knew that if I were to make any claim I would need to go to hospital straight from work or I could risk having no claim at all. I went straight to accident and emergency when we got back to Taunton, and it turned out that my foot was well and truly crushed. My foot was broken in several places, and the bones had all moved around and needed to be reset. It was excruciating and seemed to take forever, but I was finally sent home about 11:00 p.m. in a semi-cast with instructions to return on Monday and see the orthopedic specialist.

It was agony, and the added worry about money was not helping. I knew that Lisa was also worrying, and I was concerned about her and the kids. At this point, I had no idea how bad my foot was and I thought I would be back to work in about six weeks. I want to name the person who helped me next personally, because it blew me away that anyone would do this for me. A good friend named Sid whom I had known since I was a kid was visiting one day shortly after the accident and overheard Lisa telling me how worried she was about some bills we had. I did not even know he had heard, and when I reentered the front room, he simply asked what was happening with my wages. I answered him, explaining what my boss had said about the claim and why they didn't pay anymore.

He left shortly afterward, asking whether I would be about later, to which I just laughed and pointed at my foot, which was still in a big cast. It was about tea time when he returned and placed an envelope on my chest. He simply said, "Give me it back in one lump when your claim is settled." I opened the envelope to find 2,500 pounds in cash. It was amazing and I was speechless. I called Lisa in from the kitchen and explained what Sid had done, and she broke down crying. I had no idea just how worried she had been up until that moment. I can never thank Sid enough for what he did that day, and if this book becomes a bestseller, I will try and treat him someday to repay him properly. We had a really good Christmas, and we were not worried at all; of course, we were still convinced that I would be back to work in January.

I went back to see the orthopedic specialist at the end of December, and they sent me to have the cast off and have some x-rays done. I knew something was not right as soon as they took the cast off; it felt the same as it did when I had broken it originally. The x-rays confirmed what I thought and showed that my foot was still very much broken and was swelling up again almost immediately. The doctor was perplexed and you could see it, and this was the first time that CRPS (complex regional pain syndrome) was mentioned. This diagnosis was not confirmed for some time, but it was explained in brief as a condition normally associated with women. It basically meant that after traumatic injury, the injured area and the nervous system seemed to be unable to reestablish communication.

My bones would heal at a much slower rate and soft tissue damage would be ongoing and extremely painful. I was kept off work for several more weeks before I was diagnosed with CRPS properly, and by now we were getting worried. I had not been paid since before Christmas, and the money from Sid was not going to last forever. We did eventually, after seeing Dr. Nichols, the pain specialist, get a formal diagnosis of CRPS, and I was informed that I would be unable to return to any kind of physical work or indeed exercise for quite some time. My foot was continuously sore and would swell to about twice its size every single night. It was hell because I couldn't let anyone or anything touch it when it was swollen, and walking was a nightmare. I was told to buy a walking stick and to make myself walk on the foot normally to prevent long-term damage to other areas, but this was excruciating and would seriously limit what I could do in a day.

I was devastated. It just seemed so unfair that I had finally paid for all my own qualifications to get a good job and now I was unable to work. I thought it was karma and that it must be my punishment for all the horrible things I had done. Worst of all, I had to go in town and claim incapacity benefit, industrial injuries, and housing benefit. I was gutted.

I was very nearly crying when I left the doctor's office after the diagnosis. I felt like I had been physically slapped. I didn't have a clue what I was going to do, and I was angry with the whole world again. I was horrible to live with, and I was getting increasingly angry with everyone. I knew I was in danger of losing the plot if I didn't get help somewhere, and so I went back to the pain clinic and asked for some psychological help with the anger I was feeling. Dr. Nichols referred me to a psychologist to deal with the injury, but she in turn referred me to the mental health team in town.

It did me good to start talking to people about what I was thinking and also to be given some explanations regarding why I was thinking and feeling the way I was. The anger was understandable, but I needed to understand that the feelings of it being some kind of external force making me pay for past mistakes were nonsense. I was not unlucky—no more than anyone else is anyway. I was big enough to be told that the world wasn't a fair place and that bad things happened to good people all the time—and the man I met was not afraid to tell me. Steve was brilliant, and we worked together for about six months. We looked at every aspect of my life, past and present, and we tried to identify any other areas that might be affecting my anger.

We talked about my family and how they impacted on my life—and also, more importantly, how I let them. This was interesting, as I had never looked at anything like this before. It was liberating to meet someone who was not just going to nod and agree that I was right to be angry and tell me the world wasn't fair and that someone should pay. I needed someone to be blunt with me and to make me realize that it was me who decides how my disability affects me, not the world. I do not want to go into the work I did with Steve, as this was and is quite personal, and I think some things are not for sharing. But let's just say that I would advise anyone who is thinking about doing something similar to do so. It was cognitive analytical therapy (CAT) that we did, and it was amazingly effective. I did not even realize at the time how effective it was; it is the amazing things I have done since then that prove it.

I have actually reflected back on this time in my life probably more than any other. I think it is because I still cannot see where the change happened. All I know is that I finished those sessions a completely different man than I was when I began. Lisa and my kids have been fortunate enough to see this change, and I know that they are as grateful to Steve as I am. I think I want to be able to pinpoint the exact moment of change in the hope of being able to replicate it with the young people I now work with; however, I also realize that what worked for me will not necessarily work for others in the same way.

LIFE AFTER CAT

IT WAS DURING my work with Steve that I began to see another future for myself. I began thinking about going into the health and safety industry. This was partly due to the treatment I had received as an employee on the roads, but it was also a good career choice, as I had lots of experience of different kinds of job. I knew that they were seeking older applicants, and so I began to believe that I might well still have a future.

It had been nearly twelve months since I had crushed my foot, and I wanted to try and achieve something before the end of the year. My kids had watched me stop still except for hospitals for a year, and they needed to see me pull myself up and out of the rut I had found myself in. I couldn't think of anything to do for days, but then it hit me: I would give up smoking. I went to the doctor and got nicotine patches that would help me to give it up, and Lisa's sister gave me what I think was a Mavis Beacon typing course to give me something to do with my hands.

It worked. I gave up smoking in November 2004, and I was typing within a few days. I felt amazing for the first time in ages, and I knew that everyone else thought I wouldn't be able to do it, which made it all the sweeter. I had been smoking since I was a young boy (about eleven, if I remember rightly), and I couldn't believe how quickly things like my asthma got better. It was exactly what I needed, and it worked as a massive self-esteem boost.

I decided that I wanted to keep going with teaching myself, and so I enrolled in a computer course with Learn Direct, which I flew through. I loved it, and I seemed to have a great taste for learning at the time, so I kept going and enrolled in several other Learn Direct courses over the coming months. I completed everything I could find on health and safety right up to management level, but I eventually found out that to work for the HSE (Health and Safety Executive), I would have to have a degree level of education.

This was a devastating blow, as I never believed for one minute that I could do a degree, let alone be able to fund one. However, what it did do was make me want to at least inquire as to whether this was possible. I started by looking into the Open University and the kinds of courses available to me on there. I did not manage to find a way straight to a degree that would not involve me going back and doing some basics again, but I did find the perfect course for my situation.

It was a course entitled "Open to Change": a sixteen-week openings course that just looked at change and the impact it can and sometimes does have on people. I found it fascinating that something that seemed so normal could even have a course developed around it. I thought I understood what change meant and how we all just learn to adapt and overcome, but what I learned was that the lessons I had experienced as a child were very hard lessons to learn and that some people never manage to learn these skills. I learned that my reasoning skills were as good as, if not better than, the person who wrote the course. I do not mean this to sound big-headed; what I mean is that it helped me to see that actually I had plenty of transferable skills and that maybe, just maybe, I was capable of big thoughts such as perhaps going to university.

I completed the course in record time (about eight weeks, I think), and they even sent my final piece of work back, as I had submitted it too early. I had a great relationship with my tutor, who helped me a great deal, especially with things like my confidence as a person and in my writing skills. It was my tutor who advised me to go to my local colleges to find out about university courses rather than staying with the Open University, as she believed that the social side of college and university would help me gain the confidence and social skills I would need if I was to succeed in life and work away from the highways and building sites I was used to. It turns out she was right—mixing and working with the middle classes would turn out to be harder than I had ever imagined.

I was terrified at the thought of going to college. I had absolutely no knowledge of further education at all. I really believed that if I was to go back, I would have to join a group of sixteen-year-olds straight out of school; I didn't even know that adult access courses existed. I went to Somerset College for a chat with one of the learning support workers, and we discussed what I would like to do. I surprised myself by saying that I would like to try and get involved with working with young people in care or in custody again, with my fall-back plan being the HSE. They were really helpful and explained all the different avenues that they could offer, and all seemed really positive until I said that I was on incapacity benefit. Apparently, if I was able to go to college, then in the eyes of the government I could go to work, and so college funding was not available to me.

This was, of course, another devastating blow, and I very nearly went back home ready to rant about how the system was set up to stop the likes of me from getting on with my life, when I had a thought: maybe the people in charge had never actually thought about it. I went home and straightaway contacted the incapacity benefit people and arranged a meeting the following day. The college was indeed correct, and if I wanted to go to retrain, it would not be funded by the state. I explained that I was still under the hospital and that I would not be able to return to physical work ever and so I would need to retrain in some way. I also explained that I didn't even know what I could or couldn't do work-wise yet, as my pain and psychological problems were still being treated.

It made no difference to them whatsoever. The woman I was speaking to just kept repeating that if I could go to college I could go to work. I was getting angry, and so rather than argue, I used my head and asked for her boss's contact details. She offered me the number of her line manager, who would simply requote what I had already been told. I said that she misunderstood and I actually meant the head man at incapacity benefit—the man who makes the decisions. She seemed visibly shocked that I wanted this information and seemed more interested in whether I intended to complain about her than my own genuine reasons. But I put her mind at rest and explained that I simply would like to explain my situation and ask if special arrangements could be made.

She gave me his address, which I took home, and I began to compose my letter. I explained what had happened to me and the situation I found myself in work-wise, and what it was that I would like to do. I explained about the system and how I thought it was flawed, as it prevented people who needed to retrain and get back to work from actually doing so—unless, of course, they just accepted any job that was on offer, which could actually make any depression or withdrawal much worse.

It took me a few weeks to get it right and then to be brave enough to send it, but eventually I had to see whether people do actually listen. I was amazed when a couple of days later I received a reply; it read brilliantly, and I couldn't wait to show Lisa. He said that he admired me for writing the letter and my drive to improve things for my family and myself. He said that he was going to review the current guidelines and see whether things could be changed in the future. More importantly, however, he gave me permission from the top to remain on incapacity benefit for three years whilst I retrained at college. I couldn't believe it. I went straight to Somerset College with the letter to enroll in the Access to Social Sciences course beginning that September. I was finally going to be a student at thirty-three years of age (it really is never too late!).

I don't know if anyone had ever done what I had done in writing my letter, but I do know that several people have since been encouraged to do so and have been just as successful. The college wanted me to sit some adult numeracy and literacy exams to prove I was capable of working at that level, which I was happy to do rather than produce the exams I had received in jail. They had prison names stamped all over them, and I was in no hurry to show them to anyone. I wanted to start from scratch, and I had all the work I had done with Learn Direct and the Open University to get me a place.

I was terrified when September came, and I had to battle hard with myself to get the confidence to at least go and have a look. I was so pleased that I did, as everyone there was as nervous as I was. We were all introduced to each other, and most of us had pretty similar goals and aspirations. I made some good friends in the Access year who hopefully will be friends for life. I hated all the getting-to-know-you games they make you play at the beginning, but I can see now how well thought out they actually are and how well they break down barriers and actually encourage you to relax and have a laugh. I think my next biggest hurdle was my nerves and keeping them under control, as I tended to rant when nervous and sometimes I maybe disclosed a bit too much about myself.

I soon settled into it, though, and actually found myself thoroughly enjoying every minute. I was achieving quite well, and my marks were all right considering. I had some great tutors, and all were very supportive. I loved pre-social care, sociology, and psychology, but it was statistics that was going to be my problem. I was always all right at math at school, but this was a different level and it frightened me just looking through the handbook. The tutor was excellent, though, and helped me to get my head around the bits I was struggling with, and we all helped each other out as well. I became friends with three members of the group in particular: Vicky, Steve, and a young lad named Mark.

It has always fascinated me how people tend to form their own little groups, and the fact that I had made friends at all was brilliant. I must add that I was friends with everyone on the course and we all got on really well, but it was Vicky and the others whom I tended to eat with and so on. I was amazed at how much I was drawn toward sociology, especially as I had never even thought about it before the course. I had the sociology tutor as my personal tutor as well, which was helpful.

He was an excellent lecturer and managed to give all of us a taste for sociology and the changes that have happened over the past two hundred years. We looked at the health care and education systems, and I was fascinated. I found originally that I seemed to be drawn to the Marxist point of view (funny enough) that the state was taking too much control. However, I am pleased to say that I was able to begin thinking a little bit further than the end of my nose. I could see how difficult it must have been to have to make the kinds of decisions that governments had to make. It was changes in the global market and industrialization that led to many of the societal changes that the UK has been through, but the changes to people's way of living have led to a fragmentation of British culture and communities that may never be able to be remedied.

Right, I am digressing again, sorry. As you can tell, I still really like talking about sociology and I could still find myself going this way in my career at some point. I also loved psychology, and although I thought this would have been more what I was drawn to, it turned out to be mostly what I had expected. I loved learning about the impact our childhood and family have on our personalities and future aspirations and so on, but I also found it very arguable. And if everything was still so open to debate, I found it hard to see how people could be diagnosed and treated for conditions when there was also a school of thought to say that the knowledge or diagnosis materials used were flawed.

As I know so many people who have lived their lives based on what a psychologist had told them was wrong with them, I was surprised that something so debatable is used in court cases and other important forums. I did really enjoy looking at the different schools of thought, and I even found myself drawn to a particular school, namely Humanistic psychology (based on Maslow's hierarchy of needs) as this seemed to be the most logical. But I decided pretty soon into the course that psychology was not the way I wanted to go. I think, though, that writing this book has actually reinforced my thoughts on Maslow, as I think I can see that in my own case I certainly couldn't move on in life until certain basic needs that I was denied as a child had been met.

Something else I did around this time was to go and speak to the voluntary sector about offering my services, as I was told that it would help my university application. I had no idea how much this would take over my life for the next few years or how useful it would be regarding my own future working career. I was put in touch with the Youth Offending Team (YOT), which was pleased to have me on board, and I began by doing things like "Appropriate Adult," which is a service for young people in police custody, and also things like "Up2u" days that we did with young people on the verges of offending. I loved doing these, and it was fascinating hearing how little young people actually knew about the paths they were choosing and where they may lead. I enjoyed educating them about the realities, and hopefully, I managed to put them off slightly.

I would also eventually do Restorative Justice (RJ) training with YOT, and this would become my whole focus during my degree and probably throughout my life. Restorative justice involves bringing victim and offender together to talk about any incidents and also to try and repair any harm done. I could talk about this for hours, but that is for another book, I think. I was, however, asked to work as volunteer at a local emotional and behavioral difficulties school in Taunton to try and help them implement RJ into the school and to work as a mentor with some of the boys there.

I was really enjoying studying and volunteering at the school when life came back with another major blow. My nephew Kai, who was eight at the time, was diagnosed with non-Hodgkin lymphoma, a form of cancer. It was devastating to the whole family, and as always my family managed to get it totally wrong. My eldest brother, Kai's dad, went straight to Thailand, declaring that he couldn't handle it, knowing that my nephew's mum was heroin dependent and so was her new boyfriend. And so Lisa and I stepped in to take care of Kai.

I was glad I had college to take my mind of things, and so I didn't let what was happening with Kai take over everything. We (Lisa and I) took the lead with Kai, and we arranged with the hospital to keep us informed and that we would make sure that he was taken to appointments and so on. His mum was devastated, and although I normally have zero tolerance when it comes to heroin, I found myself feeling for her and supporting her as best I could. Her sister, however, was a nightmare. She was forever in the hospital whilst off her head; she even borrowed hospital gowns at one point and was wandering around like a nurse. I hated her, if I am honest. She was always saying inappropriate things around the kids or parents. I thought she should be asked to leave, but as a maternal auntie, the hospital wouldn't do it.

Eventually, I did it myself. I had arrived on the children's cancer ward in Bristol's children's hospital one morning to hear the aunt's voice from the main doorway. As I was walking toward the ward door, I could hear her arguing with someone, but it wasn't until I got close that realized exactly what she was doing. I heard her demanding that her boyfriend be released from prison because her nephew was dying! She was on the phone to Dorchester prison. I was fuming, as she was shouting this all over the ward, and all the other parents and kids were watching. The ward sister saw me arrive and asked me if I could do anything. Poor Kai was standing beside her crying, and I asked a nurse to take him to his room.

I grabbed hold of his auntie's arm and put the phone down. She stared at me, and I think she thought about saying something but the look on my face must have convinced her not to bother. I led her off the ward, and I had to prevent myself from physically hurting her. Instead, I explained to her quite clearly that (a) Kai was not dying, and (b) if she showed up on that ward again off her head on anything, I would break my rule of never hitting a woman. I made her cry, as I was quite cruel about what she looked and smelled like, but it needed to be said and, to be honest, ended up having the desired effect. They all still showed up on drugs at times, but they kept it well hidden from everyone else on the ward and they tended to leave when we arrived.

I was using all the time Kai was in hospital for my studying, and I tried my best to keep Kai doing some kind of learning as well. I spent every other night with him when he was up in Bristol, and we took him out as often as we could. He suffered awful side effects from his treatment, but he was incredibly brave. We love him dearly. He still spends a lot of time with us, and he is just like one of our own. We include him in family photos and holidays, which we know he likes. Unfortunately, his mum is still dependent and is constantly in and out of custody, and so we are an escape for Kai and a little bit of normality. We have never made him stay with us, and he likes to go home and see his brothers and his mum when she is well, although he doesn't like his step-dad at all.

It was about now that we finally got offered a larger house by the council. It was a three bedroom semi-detached house in a lovely little village called Kingston St Mary. We could not believe they were offering it to us; it was like the last great council house on the planet. We had views that stretched for miles in every direction. We could see Wellington Monument from our front room. We had what felt like half an acre of land around the front, side, and back of the house for the kids (although it was still an orchard when we moved in). Moving was hard work, especially with everything else going on, but Lisa and I believed that this was the change we had been waiting for.

On top of all this and in the middle of an Access year, God or whoever is in charge thought they would push me a little bit further. I awoke in the middle of March to discover that our little dog Nipper had passed away. I was devastated, and it felt like losing a child. To top the day off, I had to go into college and have all my Access year work signed off on by an external moderator. I went into college about midday, and returned home about 4:00 p.m. to a house full of kids. I had a lot of stuff from the garden that needed to be burnt, and so I set about building a bonfire. We had only moved in three weeks before.

The fire burnt quite fast due to the wind where we lived, and so I was soon inside keeping an eye on the bonfire ashes and having a cup of tea with Lisa when we were alerted to the smoke alarm going off upstairs. I ran up to see what was up, thinking that we had left a window open, only to find them all closed. There was a fine layer of smoke across the whole ceiling, and I could hear something crackling in the loft space. I lifted the loft hatch very slowly to see flames whipping through the loft. I got down quickly, remembering the film *Backdraft* in the 1990s and how dangerous opening a door to fire can be.

I ran downstairs and started getting everyone out and safely away from the house. It was quite surreal, because I didn't really know what to do. I ran back into the house several times and picked nothing up. I just kept running in and out until finally hot embers started landing on me. Lisa had called the fire brigade, and they started to arrive after about fifteen minutes. It was terrifying how quickly the fire took over within that fifteen minutes; three houses were now alight, and it would take seven hours to put the fire out.

We lost everything, and I mean everything—my house and my dog in one day, not to mention a year's worth of work from college. I was so pleased that I had already had it signed off that day, or I would have had to redo the lot. We were insured luckily, but to be honest that was of no consolation the following morning when we awoke in a local hotel with absolutely nothing. We did not even have a clean set of clothes or a buggy for Aidan. It was half-term, so we didn't have to worry about college or school for the kids, but we didn't know where to start.

We rang the council to find out what to do about housing, but as soon as they discovered we had insurance, they said they couldn't help and we would have to speak to our insurers. I must say that Lloyds-TSB was brilliant; as soon as we rang them, they instantly transferred some money into our account so that we could start replacing things. It turned out that our insurance covered accommodation as well, so we would be able to keep our council house tenancy whilst they rebuilt it and our insurance would rent us somewhere whilst the work was being done.

It took several weeks before we found a suitable house, and in the meantime, we moved to a more comfortable hotel where the kids could use the swimming pool and other amenities to take their minds off what they had lost, which was everything they had ever had—all their cuddly toys they had accumulated throughout the years, not to mention their favorite games and clothes. It was a very traumatic time, and we still had Kai in hospital in Bristol to deal with. However, it helped us put things into perspective, and we did eventually find a house in an area called Galmington, in Taunton, and so things began to feel a bit more normal again. We were trying to refurnish the house as we went, but as the house we were in was much smaller, we had to make do with rental furniture for a while.

We were trying to get the kids to write lists of what they had lost, but they were finding it really difficult, as with each memory came more emotion. It was an incredibly hard time for us all, and to top it off, my mum's bloke managed to end up under a lorry coming back from seeing Kai one day. Thankfully, college was coming to an end, but it was still a welcome relief from reality when I was there. People kept saying that they didn't know how I could cope so well with Kai and then the fire, but college was what made me cope—it was my escape, and when it ended and reality hit, I very nearly didn't make university at all.

There were a million reasons to put university off for a year, and everyone was telling me that I should. The problem was that I had actually felt the stress hit me when college finished. Studying seemed to be good for me.

Before, all the things I mentioned above would have been enough to drive me to the pub or even to drugs; I would have jumped on the "life's a bitch" bandwagon and switched off. I would have thought that I had lost my home and my foot, and even when I was trying to get it right, bad shit just kept happening. I know myself well enough to know that I would have used it as an excuse to not bother trying, figuring that shit would just keep happening to make it impossible.

One more setback was about to happen, though, that would actually give me a reason to stay focused. My very good friend Jamie from all those years ago in Brooklands was killed in a police chase. To top it off, he was actually involved in a head-on collision that killed another friend named Ricky. The police were following him after a hit-and-run accident he had been involved in when he tried to overtake another vehicle on a blind bend. The car coming the other way had Ricky in it, and they both died instantly. I was at college when the phone call came through, and the news actually made me fall over in the corridor. I thought it was a mistake at first, as Jamie was living quite clean at the time, but it was not to be and I would have two funerals to deal with while I finished up my first year of college.

I had learned through Kai and then the dog and the fire that actually having something to keep my mind off the misery worked for me. I had managed to achieve my Access certificate through all this adversity, and I was really proud of myself. I had been accepted at Exeter University to Childhood and Youth Studies, BA Honors. It was a three-year course, and I was determined to do it at Exeter, as I wanted to go to university not just a local college so that I could say that I had been to university. This meant a lot to me, as I had waited a long time to get into higher education and I wanted the full experience.

Kai was now responding well to treatment, I had gotten my results back from Somerset College that assured my place at Exeter, and we were starting to settle into our new house. When we moved back again, the kids made us change rooms around so that it was all different from before the fire, which we understood, but it meant Lisa and I were in the smallest bedroom of the house.

I enrolled at Exeter to begin in October 2006. I couldn't wait. I decided that I wanted to do my full motorbike license, as it would be cheaper for commuting, and Lisa agreed. I did my lessons and then my test in Taunton, and my first big proper bike was a Suzuki Bandit 600 cc. I absolutely loved it and couldn't keep off it. I was out all day everyday riding and getting used to having it before university started in October. Unfortunately for me, the good times, as always, didn't last for long, as I had an accident and wrote the bike off within a month.

I should have accepted this as an omen, but I just put it down to experience and then bought another bike with the insurance money. Lisa was a little more apprehensive about the second bike, but I convinced her that I would be more careful and she was fine. However, I ended up crashing this one as well—into a field, if I remember rightly.

I was getting really excited and nervous about university, as it was all becoming a bit close and I knew that I was going to know no one on the course and that I would be one of the oldest. I am not sure to this day why this mattered, but for some reason it was massive. I was determined to start confident and to not make the same mistakes I made at college: disclosing too much about myself and indulging in nervous ranting. I was scared that I couldn't cut it with the middle classes and that I would stand out like a social experiment of some kind. All these thoughts were not helping—but not to worry, as God was about to ensure that they were the least of my concerns.

I was traveling home one evening in the summer when I was behind a camper van that braked suddenly. I was forced to swing around it when I discovered the reason for the sudden braking. The car in front of the camper had turned right without indicating and was mid-turn when I circled the camper. I hit the car side on, and so no matter how I explained it to the insurance, it was my fault. The bike was a write-off and I was pretty injured, but I was released that day from hospital and had to rethink traveling to and from Exeter.

As it was not my fault, I was not put off riding, and I soon got myself another bike and started commuting to Exeter. It was nowhere near as hard as I had been anticipating, and I was certainly not the oldest or indeed the only mature student. I met a couple of the other lads on the course and instantly felt at home. It was brilliant because I settled straight in and my nerves were not a problem. That was, until I wrote a third bike off, and this time it was sort of my fault.

Lisa was adamant this time that I did not get another bike, and to be honest, whilst I was still in pain, I was in full agreement. The problem was that hurting heals, and when the pain had gone, so had the fear. The accident was not *all* my fault—in my eyes, anyway—and there was no way I could afford to run a second car, so my options weren't many. I was due back at university in a matter of days, and I knew that if I was going to manage traveling to and from Exeter, then I would need to do so by bike.

I told Lisa that I would like to do an advance riding course with the police and that I would then like to try biking again. We talked about it for several days, and eventually Lisa agreed to me doing that further training. I enrolled in an immediate course and had my training done within a week. I completed the training on a Thursday, picked up my new bike on Friday, and my life was changed forever on Saturday. I had done brilliantly on the training, and the police officer who taught me told Lisa that I was one of the best students he had ever had. And my new bike was an endurance bike, not a racer like the Bandit; it was a Suzuki Freewind 650 cc, and I loved it.

That Saturday was New Year's Eve 2006, and I was out practicing what I had learned on the advance training when it started raining. I remembered something that the officer had said during the training about people in cars not seeing people on bikes in bad weather, and so I decided to call on Lisa's sister and have a cup of tea until the rain stopped. I waited for about thirty minutes, and when the rain had stopped, I said my good-byes and left. I was driving out of Wellington (where Lisa's sister lives) and toward Taunton when it happened: a female driver drove straight off her drive into my path.

I can remember seeing the car move off the driveway and thinking that she was going to stop, but the next thing I knew, I was coming around on the side of the road.

I knew when I was lying there that this one was different: I couldn't move many parts of my body and the pain was excruciating. I lay there for several minutes listening to people around me talking, and I can remember asking someone to call my wife. I was really scared this time, and to be honest, I thought I was going to die.

In time, the ambulance and other emergency services arrived and were asking me all kinds of questions. I can also remember the woman who had hit me saying something about not seeing me and how devastated she was—I just thought she should try it from my side. I was put on a spinal board and taken to Musgrove Park Hospital in Taunton. By this time, someone had managed to get my phone out of one of my pockets and so Lisa was also waiting at the hospital for me. I was in a bad way, and Lisa's face confirmed this when she saw me.

I was taken straight into an emergency room, and they all started cutting my bike gear off. By this time I had been given some morphine, and so things were a bit hazy to say the least. I can remember being asked where it hurt and just saying everywhere. I was coughing up blood, which was scaring me and the medical team, and Lisa was asked to wait outside for a moment. They did a scan there and then, and discovered that my liver had been lacerated and I was bleeding quite heavily internally. I was put on the emergency surgery list just in case.

I was in a lot of pain still, and I couldn't move my arms or legs for a long time. I knew that some things were broken and that I would need x-rays, but I was not ready for just how much. My right arm was broken in about three places, my wrist was on top of my hand, and my radial head had completely broken off in my elbow. They had to reset it about three times, which didn't help much. My right foot, which already had the CRPS, was unrecognizable—just like a ball on the end of my leg. My shoulder was also really painful, but because of the internal bleeding and the fact that I was so largely built, they had trouble x-raying inside my shoulder and so it was left for a later date (they thought that my arm had simply dislocated and reset itself during the accident). I was worrying about university and all the other things in my life, and to be honest, I started thinking that life was out to ***k me up one way or another.

I was kept on the ward for about a week, and then I was allowed home. It was decided that my liver would heal itself and that the bladder and other problems I was experiencing would probably do the same. I was in a full-arm cast and it weighed a ton, although I was not mobile anyway. My foot was still massive, and so walking was out of the question, and my arm was too heavy to even move. Time passed quite quickly when I was at home, and it was then that I started worrying that things were not getting any better.

My arm was too heavy to even lift, and as a weight lifter I knew that this was not right. And I was peeing like an old man, sometimes taking up to five minutes to go. My foot was not getting smaller as it normally did with the CRPS, and that was scaring me as well. I was finally due to see the orthopedic specialist, and he seemed to be quite concerned about the fact my bones didn't seem to be healing well. He asked me to see the pain specialist again to see whether he thought CRPS was to blame, which I arranged.

I was left in a semi-cast because of the weight and waited until I could see Dr. Nichols. My foot was still massive after about nine weeks, and I was still unable to walk or even wear shoes, and so hospital visits were a nightmare. It was about this time that I realized something was seriously wrong with my arm. I awoke to find that my arm had dropped out of its socket; it was hanging down and quite limp. I was seriously worried and told Lisa to get me straight to the hospital, which she did. I went to see Dr. Nichols, as I knew he would see me. I was not at all ready for what he was going to say.

His face said a lot as soon as I showed him my arm. He looked like *he* wanted to cry, let alone me. He looked at my arm and shoulder, and then said something that I will never forget. His exact words were: "I am so sorry, Declan, but I think that you have damaged a nerve in your shoulder." He also said, "I hope that I am wrong, because if you have done the damage that I think you have, then you may have lost the use of your right arm."

I was in shock, and I had to ask him what he meant. He explained that if I had gotten serious nerve damage, then I would need a serious operation, but more importantly, I would never be lifting weights again with that arm. Any movement that an operation might provide would be minimal.

I couldn't quite take it in. What did he mean, I had lost my right arm? How could that be when it was still there? To be honest, I don't think I wanted to understand. It was easier to live in blissful ignorance—and that would remain the same for some time. I was sent back to the orthopedic specialist to see what he thought, and he confirmed Dr. Nichols' fear and sent me to see a nerve specialist named Dr. Sinisi in the Royal National Orthopaedic Hospital in Stanmore, London. He was an incredible man, and I liked him immediately. He was ranting about the NHS and how he hated it. He did, however, confirm my worst fears: that my nerve was almost certainly damaged and he would have to do an exploratory operation to be sure.

He told me that it would be about two weeks until the operation, and he explained that if he did indeed find nerve damage, he would try and repair it whilst he was inside me. He explained that if the nerve was severed, it would need a graft, and that he would remove the nerves from my forearm to use, as they were the easiest. He explained that I would lose the feeling in my forearm but that it should not really affect anything else. He also confirmed what Dr. Nichols had said about my training days being over, regardless of the operation. He told me not to expect the operation to fully repair my shoulder, as it very rarely did. It turned out that I was a bit of a rarity, as most people who sever their brachial plexus (the shoulder nerve I had damaged) died, as their neck would be broken. As it turned out, it was all the weight lifting I had done in my life that had actually saved me.

I was incredibly nervous about the operation, but I was the eternal optimist and I refused to believe that I would not get better. I was sure that the operation would be quite a simple one, and the way that Dr. Sinisi had explained things made me think it would be like keyhole (laparoscopic) surgery. How wrong I was! I made the mistake of going up to London for the operation on my own, as it seemed easier. I arrived early and was placed straight onto the ward. I had a single room, which was nice, but I must say that even though Stanmore is indeed the best hospital in the world at what it does, it is a little bit behind the times. There were no televisions or radios, and so I was resigned to reading as much as I could to take my mind off the operation.

The operation was planned for the following morning, and so I was nil by mouth (could no longer eat or drink) and got an early night. I slept surprisingly well and awoke to find a gown and surgical underwear on the bed. The operation would either be very short or several hours, depending on what they found inside. Dr. Sinisi came to see me again before the operation and answered all my questions, and that was it—I was in the theater. As it turned out, it was the longer operation and I was in surgery for about five hours. I awoke in the recovery room and I was very sick. They gave me nearly every anti-sickness drug they had before I could return to the ward.

I was devastated. I looked to my right and it looked like I had two pieces of bacon stapled together on my shoulder. I had about a hundred staples running from my neck to my elbow, and I also had blood running down the back of my head. I called for a nurse to tell her about my head, and she informed me that I had came back from surgery like this and that someone had dropped my head on the operating table. I had to laugh.

I think I was in shock. I was genuinely expecting to wake up and find a little one—or two-inch-long scar, not an eighteen-inch monstrosity. It was horrible, and if ever I needed Lisa, it was then. I was hundreds of miles from home, and I never felt more alone than I did that day. I told the nurse that I was leaving and to get me a taxi. I think she thought I was joking until I started trying to get dressed. I know it was a little stupid, looking back on it, but I wanted my Lisa and my kids around me.

The sister reluctantly got me a taxi (after making me sign about twenty liability waivers), and I went to Paddington to get a train to Taunton. I was pumped full of morphine and other painkillers, and so I probably looked to everyone else like some kind of junkie, but I didn't care. I almost forgot to mention the fact that my right arm was strapped to me in what is called a hunter sling (and would be for the next nine weeks, continuously).

I managed to get onto a train and travel back to Taunton, where I knew Lisa was waiting for me. The train seemed to shake me all over the place and it was excruciating. By the time I arrived in Taunton, I had blood dripping down my arm and running off my hand. I would like to add how brilliant people were on the train, getting me drinks and tissues. Someone even carried my bags out to the front of the station for me. I managed to make it to the car before it hit me hard. I cried all the way home and didn't speak at all. When we got in the house, I showed Lisa my shoulder and arm, and she knew straightaway why I was so upset.

The problem may well just seem like vanity, but it wasn't. When I was younger, I was extremely small, and I truly believe that it was one of the reasons I felt the need to be so violent and carry weapons. And so I started training really young to try and get bigger. It took me years to get to a size that I was comfortable with. I worked hard and started looking after myself. Self-esteem is something that I never really understood back then, but now I understand completely. My size had become my security blanket. I liked that I was fit and strong, and I was very good winding my friends up who were big drinkers and already had beer bellies and so on. I was determined to still look good in my fifties, and I did at least an hour's training every day.

I think when I looked at those staples, I knew it was all over and that I was not ever going to be me again—not the me I had come to rely on, anyway. I hated how it looked, and there was nothing that anyone could say that was going to make me feel better. I was signed off from university, but I didn't want to be at home overthinking things, and so within a week I was going to Exeter by train. I even showed up for a test condition essay, but they sent me home saying that I would need to have a right hand to write. I hadn't thought about that bit.

I bought myself a voice recorder so that I could record lectures and seminars, and I also bought Dragon voice recognition software to help with writing. I was determined that I would not be dropping out of university, no matter how sensible the option might seem. I had waited thirty years to get there, and I was not about to give up. I managed to finish my first year with a Dean's commendation for outstanding achievement, but I knew that I would need help to finish with a good mark overall. I got in touch with the disability resource center, and they were amazing. They managed to get me funding for a scribe and also provided me with a mentor/counselor for myself whom I found really useful. I used our time every week to talk about everything that was going on, and it meant that I was not carrying it around with me.

As a family, we had had a mental couple of years and it seemed never-ending. I was really worried about how I would cope if my arm never recovered and also about things like my own image around town. I started seriously worrying about things like safety, and I felt very vulnerable indeed. I even started wondering whether Lisa would still want to be with me if I could not protect her and our family, as I believed that this was why she was with me originally.

I would have to get used to hospitals, as I would be spending a lot of time in them over the coming years. I was still suffering from bladder problems, and I was having tests for that in Taunton, as well as beginning an intensive physiotherapy program that would involve hydro—and physiotherapy sessions three times a week at Musgrove. I went every time, believing that it was for the greater good and "no pain, no gain," as they say.

I was also still seeing Dr. Nichols about all the associated pain problems I was experiencing. He was being really honest with me about the prognosis, and I appreciated this a lot, as everyone else seemed to be afraid to tell me. He referred me to a psychologist to try and help me deal with how my arm and shoulder looked and felt, as I was really struggling even looking at it in the mirror and I would not let Lisa touch it at all. I was becoming increasingly paranoid about going out, and although I knew that this was not the way to go about things, I just couldn't seem to help it.

If it hadn't been for university and my voluntary work in the school, I would have gone mad, and actually, it was the support I had from all these things that would eventually make me believe that there was a future for me after all—it just might not have been what I was originally planning. I won't pretend that I was aware of this at the time; I just knew that if I gave up, then I would be finished.

You would be amazed at how many people told me that I was a fool and that I should be staying at home, saying that I would get millions in loss of earnings. It is funny, but I would probably have said that same thing to one of my mates in the same situation. But when it is you in the spotlight, suddenly you have to think things through. I had three kids watching me, and how I reacted to setbacks would affect how they did things themselves. I wanted my daughters and my son to see that you can overcome anything if you really want to. I had never let life stop me in my tracks, and I wasn't about to start now.

I started just trying to focus on the positives in my life, and there were many of them. I had a beautiful wife and three adorable children who loved and respected me. I had gained the respect of both the staff and students at the school where I was working as a volunteer for YOT, and I was well respected at Exeter University.

I did have a future—I just didn't quite know what it would be yet.

The problem with nerve surgery is that you have to wait a long time to get a long-term prognosis. Nerves repair at the rate of a millimeter a day, and so I had to wait several months anyway. I decided that I wanted to wait until I knew exactly where I stood before I started panicking. I think certain medical professionals thought this was denial, but it was not at all. I simply knew that the doctors didn't know what was going to happen yet, so how could I?

I was also being prepared for more surgery. The plan was to remove my radial head so as to give me more rotation in my arm. I was also told that I may need to have another nerve operation in my back, as they thought that my supra-scapular nerve was also damaged—although they did not believe that it was severed, so they wanted to wait and see if it repaired itself before they operated. I had to wait at least twelve months after the first operation because of the body trauma I had already experienced.

I kept up with my physiotherapy and all the other medical appointments, and life just plodded on for about three months. And then I was invited back up to Stanmore for a week's worth of intensive physiotherapy and also some nerve conduction tests. I was dreading it really, because I knew that reality was about to hit me hard. I went up alone and asked Lisa and the kids to follow me up in a couple of days. It was half-term, so we could do some things in London as a family in the evenings. I was on the rehabilitation ward with several other people with similar injuries, and we all had a set and full week ahead of us.

I was finally allowed out of the hunter sling. My arm was pretty weak and unresponsive when I first saw the physio, but they said it was to be expected at this point. I knew that they were being optimistic for my sake; they also thought I was in denial and tried to make me see someone else to talk about the reality. I was not in denial—I just wasn't ready to give up yet. I wanted to lift weights again and I was determined to keep trying.

The week went all right, and I met some nice people who helped me put things into perspective. We were all hurt in different ways, but we all shared some common things, such as the life-changing aspects of our injuries that we were all trying to deal with. I was seen by Dr. Sinisi, who wanted to know what was happening regarding my radial head and other injuries, but I didn't know, as I had not seen anyone. He arranged for me to see a friend of his to try and get everything dealt with in Stanmore. It was to be the beginning of the end regarding my arm, but I didn't know that at the time.

I saw an orthopedic specialist who took several x-rays of my wrist and elbow before he told me what he thought. The main problem was that my radial head was still floating in my arm and it was restricting movement.

The obvious answer was to remove the radial head, as it was not needed. However, because of the damage to my wrist during the accident, there was a chance of my forearm collapsing if it was removed. This was a devastating blow, as it meant that the movement I had in my arm and the rotation (which was already minimal) would be all that I would ever have.

On top of this, I had seen another specialist in Taunton regarding my bladder problem and I had been put on medication for that, which would also be for life. I was getting increasingly depressed now and worried. I was due to leave university for the summer, and this was worrying because I didn't want time to think.

I decided to try and find a job. It was going to be a big deal really, because I was already worried about finding a decent job with my past history, but adding my recent disability into the mix, I believed I might be unemployable, even in the care industry. I decided to look for a similar job to the one I had done before, working twenty-four-hour shifts ten times a month, which would not have affected university too much as I knew that if I offered to do all the weekends I would be sorted, because they are always hard shifts to fill. I spoke to Lisa about my plans, and she said it would be fine with her but that I needed to speak to my doctors beforehand. I agreed reluctantly because I thought they would say no, but to my surprise they were all for the idea.

My first thought was, however, to ask for work at the school where I had been working as a volunteer, but there was not anything available at the time and so I started looking properly. A job came up with a local private care company that dealt with seriously damaged young people, and I was invited along for an interview. As always, I was really nervous about the interview, as I knew I would be asked about my criminal record and so on. Although it had been nearly seventeen years since I had been in any trouble, nothing is ever spent when working with young people or vulnerable adults (and rightfully so). It was just never pleasant having to explain it all.

The interview went brilliantly and I was offered the job straightaway. I was blown away. They wanted me to come straight on board and begin to implement restorative practices throughout their care homes. I would not even be doing twenty-four-hour shifts; they wanted me available to go into homes in the evenings to defuse situations as they occurred and then to spend my work time resolving any existing issues between the young people and their carers. It was almost my perfect job, but as always, life had another plan for me.

I was due back in London to see Dr. Sinisi, and I knew that he was going to be expecting some progress. His disappointment was obvious, as nothing had improved. He was quite optimistic still, telling me that he thought that it was pain that was stopping me from progressing, and he asked for a new set of x-rays in my shoulder.

Bearing in mind that it was now nearly eighteen months since the accident and I had been having physio three times a week on my arm and shoulder, I was amazed at what was uncovered. I would also like to add at this point that when I had complained about pain in Taunton physiotherapy, I was informed that I shouldn't be feeling any pain, almost to the point of insinuating that I was lying.

The x-rays uncovered a shoulder in six pieces, a rotator cuff in three pieces, and a collarbone that was not even attached to the skeleton. As well, my scapular was broken away from my shoulder. Dr. Sinisi was fuming when I told him that I had been complaining about pain and the response I had been given. I couldn't wait to go back and see the physio myself to ask her to explain herself. When I did, I was amazed at what she said. Her only answer was that it was not their job to do x-rays, that they were meant to follow what the doctors had told them to do. I explained to her that surely she could have referred me back for an x-ray if I was complaining about pain, but her response to that was to refuse to treat me anymore—amazing!

I also had to inform my new employers that I would be unable to begin work at that point due to my injuries and that I was due to have major surgery. They were, of course, not happy about the situation, but they knew that I was unaware of these problems before the interview and so were very understanding, even offering to keep the job open for me until after the operation.

I was really unhappy with Musgrove, and I got the impression that they were inept to say the least. They had told me that they couldn't x-ray through my muscles at the time of the accident, and when I put this to other departments and hospitals, they all responded the same way: "What do we do with athletes, then, if they get injured?!" I am not about to start legal proceedings or anything like that; I just would have liked an acceptance on their part or at least an apology.

And so I was set for another piece of surgery, and this was to be a shoulder reconstruction, I was really happy in one aspect, to be honest, as my shoulder sloped off quite badly from my neck and the shoulder team had said that they probably could give me a bit more structure and posture, which I knew would help me loads. The operation was done in September 2008, just in time to start my final year at Exeter—story of my life.

The operation went well, although I was placed back in a sling for a few months. My scribe was excellent at university and made sure that all my notes were kept up to date. I did miss one assignment, but the university allowed me to be given an average mark based on the rest of the group's results, which I thought was amazingly accommodating. I was worried about my dissertation, which would be starting after Christmas, but I was assured by the hospital that I would be out of the sling by then, and I was.

I was, however, given some bad news after the operation, which would affect my employment with the care company. The surgeon who rebuilt my shoulder came to see me after the operation to tell me what he had found inside. He explained that when he went inside my shoulder, my deltoid muscle was like a veil. He explained that he had cut it in half and sewn it back up on top of itself to give me a little more support in my arm. However, he also said that due to the amount of muscle wastage that I had suffered, there was not much muscle or tissue left around my shoulder and so it would be pretty much unprotected.

He explained that the likelihood of my shoulder collapsing was very high due the lack of protection, and he had fears about me being involved in particularly violent situations, since if my shoulder did collapse again they would not be able to rebuild it. I was not sure what to do at first, but after speaking to Lisa, I was sure. Lisa asked me to look in the mirror and to think about how much better my shoulder now looked aesthetically to me and how much better my posture was. She was quite blunt when she said I had to choose whether working and losing my shoulder again would be worth it. She said I should at least give the operation a year to heal properly before I put myself at risk. And that is why I love my Lisa—for all her faults, she knows me very well, and I knew she was right in what she was saying.

I had to phone my potential new employers and inform them that it would be unsafe for me to begin work in their care homes. It was supposed to be a very sad phone call, but instead I was about to be shocked once more. The company director came on the phone and asked me whether I could come into his office for a chat. It was amazing to me—I couldn't even turn a job down easily. I went to see him the following day, and we talked for hours. It turned out that he knew exactly who I was reputation-wise and that he had run a doorman company for years. He was genuinely impressed with what I had managed to do with my life, especially as he knew my dad and the rest of my family. Eventually, we got around to talking about work and he made me an offer I couldn't refuse.

He wanted me to work for his company because he believed that all the kids he had would respond well to me. He offered my £18,000 a year to work in his school on the days that I was not at university as a mentor with the young people and also to implement restorative justice throughout his company in a more secure environment. I was, as you can imagine, speechless, except to say that I would of course take the job. I started working again in November 2008, and it would be the beginnings of a mini-adventure all of its own, which I will come back to later.

I was traveling down to Exeter by train and taxi, which was expensive to say the least, but I used the time to read and keep on top of things. I was determined to finish with at least a 2:1 and that was going to take some hard work. I was on morphine and a lot of other painkillers, which made things extremely difficult, but I couldn't do anything about that as the pain would have been a bigger distraction. Kai was getting better and was now in full remission, and so all my energies could be focused on work and university.

It seemed unfair that all of it had to be so hard, but I began to look at life as "character building stuff" and I came to believe that every day was a school day of sorts. I was starting to see strengths in myself that I never knew I had. I had always been told by other people how strong and clever I was, but they always meant physically strong and clever as in streetwise. What I was learning was different. I was mentally stronger than I ever realized, and I was being told I was academically able by really clever people. It is funny, but I think I had spent my life waiting for the blow that would finish me—not a physical blow, as they never scared me, but more of a mental blow that would have sent me to the loony bin or nuthouse.

I always thought that I was only one more nightmare away from a nervous breakdown, and I actually worried about it. I was finally beginning to believe in myself as a human being, as an equal to everyone else—not just someone who has to fight for every scrap of decent life I got, not someone who was destined to dig holes or labor to make someone else money. I was starting to realize that people wanted to listen to me and people thought I had something to say that was worth listening to. It would be this belief that got me through my final year.

I was achieving well at Exeter, and my marks were becoming consistently high enough for a 2:1, even a first if I was really lucky in my final few papers. I had a great scribe, and I only had a couple of test condition essays left to do. Most were normal assignments, which I could take my time with. The test condition essays were really hard, and I didn't get great marks in them. It was hard dictating a 3,000-word essay, and it was hard for the scribe to know when I was dictating and when I was thinking out loud as I do when I am writing myself.

I was enjoying going into work as well, although I did miss the other school that I had been volunteering in, but Lisa and I were not penniless for the first time since the accident. There were only six students, and they were lovely—although all a little messed up, as they had all been right through the care system. One of them actually had over fifty placements, and another had just been taken away from all of her siblings, who were in the process of being adopted or fostered to families all around the globe. It was heartbreaking for me to see these kids who had obviously been mistreated by a failing system, and it was hard to keep reminding myself to remain professional and keep my thoughts about the system to myself.

The first thing I did was to whistle-blow to my new boss what a sham his school was. He had asked me in the interview to be honest with him and, if I saw anything that was wrong, to keep him informed. I think he may have regretted this decision slightly. The first thing that had to be done was to sack the headmaster, who was calling the kids "numpties" and "unteachable." This, to me, was unacceptable, as no child is unteachable, and to have put-down nicknames infuriated me (remember what the Christian brothers did to me). He also had the school split into two groups based on his evaluation of their abilities, and so one group had a teacher (the functional group) and the others were just left wandering around the school bored (the dysfunctional group).

I asked my boss to sack both the headmaster and the teacher, and we put a whole new team together who could teach GCSE grade work for the older students and key stage three for the younger students (which is what they should have been studying in the first place), as well as an excellent art teacher who could come in and do art therapy a couple times a week. I also employed someone to specifically work on things like anger management and communication skills that these young people desperately needed. The kids had simply learned that if they shouted and bullied hard enough, they got what they wanted from social workers, but what I was there to teach them was that it all stops at sixteen. Social workers will give in to them, but who was going to do that for them when they left care? Did they think that the job center would give them money if they shouted? Did they think that college would let them attend if they shouted and bullied them? The answer was no, and they needed to know that.

I was not like anyone they had ever met before—I could tell. In the beginning, I didn't tell them all about my past, but as time went on, I shared things with them to help maintain a positive relationship, and it worked. Even though I challenged them when no one would, they never attacked me like they did others. I knew I was making them think about things they had never thought about before, specifically their own futures—not their mum's problems or their dad's, not what drug would be their drug of choice, not how to have a baby and get a flat. These things were really what they thought they were destined to do! They thought they would have to tell employers that they had been in care, for god's sake. I was disgusted that no one was doing any serious work with these young people; it was like they were being babysat and paid off until their sixteenth birthdays, when they would be offered a £2000 "leaving care" grant and then abandoned.

I had to stand back and watch why so-called advocates—who were employed to speak up for young people in care—would phone up every week to inform one of the girls of all the horrible things happening to her siblings and her mother because she "had a right to know." But when social services told that same girl that they were moving her to another care company without even an introduction or visit to the new home, there was not an advocate in sight. I was disgusted at the system these kids were in, and I was learning more each day.

I knew that there was no point in getting all upset about it, and my boss was no more or less happy with the system than I was. He was incredibly honest with me and was really happy for me to make all the changes I was asking for. He supported me all the way; his heart was in the right place, and he was genuinely trying to do the best he could with the young people he had in his care. He would be the first to admit that his head was for business and that he had employed people who he thought were doing things how he expected them to. I understood this point, as I myself (as I have said earlier in this book) have lied to get jobs, but I couldn't understand why anyone would go into this industry if they didn't at least care.

It is sad that people use damaged young people to pay their mortgages off, but I am afraid this is inevitable because of the system that feeds kids into the private sector and the pay that is on offer. I saw the same thing at the school where I had been before—most teachers did not and would not have chosen to work with students with emotional or behavioral difficulties, but they were offered a £10,000 bonus every three years to do so. If you don't have the empathy and understanding that working with these young people requires, you shouldn't work with them, because the impact of some of the negative comments that these people can come out with—such as how feral and uncontrollable these kids are—can have serious long-term impacts on these young people's self-image and aspirations.

I am going off subject again slightly—I do apologize, but it felt like that was a good time to mention it. I was happy in my job, I must say; the kids made it worthwhile to me. When I first started, we were lucky to get two of the students for one day a week, but within a month I had all six every day, and I was chuffed to bits, as all the carers told me they would never come. It was funny but I could already sense the same thing happening with the carers that had happened before, but this time I wasn't bothered by it, as I knew that I had done all I could to put my past behind me, and if people were still going to judge me on my childhood, then so be it. I was not about to do a shit job so as not to upset anyone else.

I started implementing restorative practices through the young people. I think it was genius, because the staff could not refuse to take part—as I had the full commitment from the management and this became a requirement. Slowly I was teaching the kids to tell me what happened in the houses that was winding them up, and my staff in the school were giving the young people the skills to be able to sit in a room and state what their problems were and to take the power back themselves. It was too easy if the carers wound them up and then they lost the plot. If the carers were winding the situation up, then I would arrange a meeting with the young person and the carers, as well as the boss. That way, the young person got to see that they were listened to, and above all, nine times out of ten when unsupported by the boss, the carers would behave like the young people used to.

However, as much as I was enjoying work, I still had university to finish, and as my dissertation deadline grew closer, the pressure started to mount. I knew what I wanted to write about—I was going to do a case study looking at the links between school exclusion and criminal or ASB (anti-social behavior). I had already spoke to the family that was going to be my case study, as I had been working with one of the sons for some time through the YOT. It was really insightful, and I was fascinated to discover that with all the research done around this area, I was one of the first people to speak to one of the families involved.

I was worried about my final mark, as I knew that I would be devastated if I got a 2:2 or less. I had worked hard, and I wanted the mark to prove it. I know that I had had massive surgery twice during the three years, but unfortunately, any future employers wouldn't know that and I didn't fancy having to make excuses every time I applied for a job. I didn't have anything else due, other than a presentation before the end of term, and so I decided that I could cope with both work and study.

I think work helped actually, because sometimes you need to switch off from an essay to be able to return to it with a clear head. The good thing about my job was that there was plenty to occupy my mind. I handed my dissertation in on the final day all bound and professional looking. I was very proud of myself—now I faced the wait for my mark, and it would be a long one.

In the meantime, my boss had informed me that his wife and family had agreed to immigrate to Canada and that he would be selling the business after the summer term. This left all of us at the school looking for work. The carers would be all right because whoever was buying the business would be keeping the care homes, but the school was to be closed. I was a little disappointed, but my boss had been more than fair with me, and he had proved to me that I was indeed employable and at a higher level than I would have thought.

I started looking for another job, but as luck would have it, the school that I used to work in as a volunteer contacted me and invited me in for a meeting. I was not sure what to expect, but it was a very promising meeting and I was asked if I would like to set up my own unit attached to the school. My main role would still be restorative practices, but I would also be responsible for establishing a social and emotional development program with my colleague from the closing school. Timing is everything on this planet, and it was finally on my side.

I was awaiting my degree results for what seemed like an eternity, but they finally arrived in May 2009. I had earned my 2:1, and I was ecstatic. I was so proud of myself that I smiled continuously for a fortnight, I am sure. My kids could finally see their dad as I had always wished them to see me: a strong, determined, and driven man who could overcome anything . . . well, almost anything. I had achieved something that I never thought would be possible—I had graduated from university.

I thought that things couldn't get any better: a county job (which, to anyone who understands, is the "holy grail" if you have a colorful past) and an excellent degree from an Ivy League university like Exeter. But then out of the blue, I was awarded another Dean's commendation for my final year. A 2:1 and two Dean's commendations . . . . that had to bring it up to a first, surely. Well, it did in my head anyway.

We really enjoyed the summer, and although I was still a little self-conscious, there was no way I was going to miss graduation. I could only get two tickets, though, which I was upset about. I decided that Lisa and I would take our eldest, as she was the next one in line for university and I think that she was proud of her dad, as she could still remember the old dad, whereas I didn't think the others could. It was a great moment, and I received my degree from an old friend from children's television named Floella Benjamin in July 2009. It was the proudest moment of my life (next to my kids being born, obviously).

CONCLUSION

I HAVE SINCE begun to work in the school in Taunton, and I am very happy there, although my end goal has now changed. My medical situation is not improving, and the prognosis is not good. I am in constant pain and my arm is pretty much useless; I cannot physically train, and I am getting fat. It is a killer, letting yourself go, and I am determined to fight it all the way. Despite this, I did my Padi diving course in Egypt last year, and my eldest wants to do hers this year so that we can dive together.

I have spoken to Exeter about doing an M.Phil/PhD, and I have asked my solicitor to ask for a four years loss of earnings to allow me to do this over the coming years. I need time to digest all the changes in my life and hopefully come to terms with my new situation. I want to publish this book, which I have also been writing over the course of my degree, and I want to think about setting up my own provision to help young people on the verges of offending behavior look at themselves in a healthier, more positive light and make positive plans for their futures.

I am even seriously considering becoming a social worker or even a developmental psychologist to try and get a better understanding of the effects our young lives have on our continuing development. One thing is certain, though—this is not the end of my education, but rather it is the beginning. I intend to become a lifelong learner and to further my knowledge in all areas regarding young people, with the hope of being able to write more books and papers that hopefully will help us improve the outcomes for disadvantaged young people all around the globe.

AFTERWORD

I AM NOT sure whether anyone else will get from this book what I have, although in the beginning I didn't know what that was myself. I started writing this as therapy for myself and because everyone told me I should, but I had no idea what it was I would get out of it. This was to be one of the most positive things I have ever done, because it has helped me see that life isn't over and it was never set in stone. Life has impacted me at every turn; sometimes it has seemed unlivable, and I nearly gave up on myself many times. The more negative choices I made, the worse life got, and when I decided that I wanted more out of life, it made me prove it.

But I have proven it. I have proven that we can turn it around given the right circumstances and we can make things happen. All we can do is keep focused and look for the opportunities that can make things happen, as they do come along. The trick is to not let all the negative things in life overshadow your future. If you need help, get it; do not be afraid to ask. Someone once told me that a man who needs to ask for help may seem stupid for a moment, but a man who never asks for help remains stupid for life. This quote has been drummed into my kids, and hopefully, it will be drummed into my grandchildren when they are around, as it has carried me (even though I didn't know it) through my younger years and into manhood.

I am glad I asked for help after my foot accident, as it changed my life. My only regret is not asking earlier. Maybe my daughters would not have missed out on a great dad when they were little and I was able-bodied enough to enjoy life with them. Money from my accident might give us opportunities now that we may never have had if not for the accident, but if I had not asked for help before this accident, this money would have been the death of me and I know it.

Thank you, Steve, for all your help and support; when I needed to see things clearly, you showed me the way. Thank you, Warwick, for helping me to believe in myself enough to go to that interview at Exeter University, as it led to me writing this. There are many more people I wish to thank, but way too many for his book. I will hopefully show you all how grateful I am by living my life to the fullest and helping as many young people as I can to do the same.

I also want to thank my wife, Lisa, and our three beautiful children who have helped me incredibly over the past eighteen years of my life, but in particular these past three years, by believing in me and supporting me in all my decisions. Lisa has always trusted me to do the right thing, and she has always encouraged me to strive for the things that are important to me. No matter how difficult life has gotten, she has never left me. I love you, Lisa, and you will never regret the confidence you have had in me. It is your turn now, and I want to help you reach your stars.

My eldest daughter has also been incredible over the past years, as she has taken a lot of my stress at times. Her sixteen years were never going to be easy with me as a dad, but she has helped me learn to trust her and also to look at my own issues when dealing with her. I am sorry for all the tears, my love, and if I could take them back, I would. You are a beautiful, intelligent young woman, and I am so proud of you it hurts. I cannot wait to see what you become over the coming years, and I will help you in any way I can.

My middle child is also a girl, and she is a star. She is a straight fives student, and she has just started secondary school in all the top groups. I am so proud of her because she has used school as her distraction from all our problems, just as I did. She has had an awful few years at her young age: dealing with Kai, the house fire, and all my accidents and consequent surgeries. Yet the way she has handled it all is incredible, and I am so pleased I could cry. I hope that you continue to achieve at the highest levels, as I know that this is what you yourself want. But no pressure, my love; I will be here to help whenever you need me.

And finally I turn to my son, who was only two weeks old when all these big changes began. I could not do much with him in the early days because of my foot, and then when he was two I lost my arm and have been unable to pick him up when he has fallen. Honestly, son, this has been breaking my heart. I will make it all up to you someday, and we will find things we can do together now that life has settled down and you are getting a little older. I am pleased you get to enjoy your football (even if it is with someone else), and as soon as you pick a team, I look forward to sitting on the terraces with you. You will be a great man one day, and I cannot wait to see it.

I am now thirty-seven years of age, and I have thirty years of working life left to live. I am hoping that my troubles are over and that this is my time to shine. Watch this space!